WS8

THE
INFLUENTIAL
WOMAN

THE
INFLUENTIAL
WOMAN

*How to achieve success
without losing your
femininity*

Lee Bryce

PIATKUS

© 1989 Lee Bryce
First published in 1989 by
Judy Piatkus (Publishers) Limited,
5 Windmill Street, London W1P 1HF

British Library Cataloguing in Publication Data

Bryce, Lee,
    The influential woman
    1. Women. Careers. Development
    I. Title
    331.7'02

    ISBN 0–86188–829–4

Cartoons by Min Cooper
Typeset in 11/12pt Linotron Ehrhardt by
Phoenix Photosetting, Chatham
Printed and bound in Great Britain by
Billings Ltd, Worcester

To my sister Gail,
whose belief in me gave me
the courage to write this book.

Many thanks to my friend and colleague Nuala Swords Isherwood for painstakingly reading through the draft manuscript and offering me invaluable advice and encouragement.

Contents

1
What makes a successful woman?

This is a book for all women who want to become successful. Success for you, as an individual, means doing so well in your own field that, by your own standards, you can feel proud of what you have done. Success for women as a whole means more women in top jobs and in positions of power.

SEX DISCRIMINATION
Women work harder, are better qualified and often more competent than their male counterparts, but do not reach senior positions with the same ease. The statistics speak for themselves. Among the 1,000 directors of the top 100 UK firms, there are only eight women, and not one is a chief executive. Fewer than 3 per cent of the directors of 1,500 British companies are women, yet women amount to nearly 45 per cent of the workforce.[1] Women still earn substantially less than men. If we compare the figures for those in full-time employment men still earn just over 50 per cent more than their female colleagues.[2] In Australia men earn 20 per cent more than women,[3] and in Canada they earn

35 per cent more.[4] This discrepancy is largely because working women tend to be clustered in the lower grades, and traditionally female occupations like social work and teaching, where they earn less. For example, in the non-industrial Civil Service women form 77 per cent of the lowest grade but only 4 per cent of the most senior grade.[3] So we lose out in comparison with men – in terms of power, seniority, and income.

What *do* we need to do to change the situation? It is obviously not enough to work very hard and get the right qualifications. We do this already. I think we need first to look at successful people and find out just what it is they do that makes *them* successful. We can then compare this with what we as women are *not* doing, to see what is holding us back.

LEARNING FROM MEN-AT-THE-TOP

The climate *is* changing for career women. Accountancy and law are just two examples of once male professions which have been invaded by women in the last few years. Computer and television companies tend to have women at professional and management level and publishing has always been an attractive industry for women.

Yet the number of women in senior positions is still low. Why is this? It is certainly not because of lack of technical skills and qualifications. Women do work hard, but often they don't work hard at the right things. I'm completely in agreement with Linda Agran, one of my interviewees, when she says, 'I'm sick of going to meetings at senior levels and seeing nothing but men in boring grey suits with white shirts and white faces!' I don't want to spend my life working hard and not reaping the rewards either! I think women need to know what it is that successful men *do* to get to the top, because we can all learn from them.

Successful men know how to make themselves visible. They perform well at meetings, are not afraid to speak up, and are capable of giving presentations. They stand up for themselves and are assertive rather than passive. They have a habit of planning their careers and setting career goals. They know how to choose a path that gives them the right visibility and experience for jobs at the top. They know how to use authority and power, and they are not afraid to wield them. Most of all, they face up to challenges and understand that you have to do frightening things and take risks from time to time.

As a rule, women do not perform well in these areas. Of course there are men who are bad at taking risks, increasing their visibility, being assertive and so on and therefore don't get to the top either. *But so few women are good at these factors!*

I think it is because we don't do these things that success eludes us, rather than that we aren't competent or hardworking enough. In fact, we often mistakenly assume that the reason we are not progressing fast enough is because we aren't sufficiently skilled and competent. We fall for the myth that women have to be better at everything and so we try to help our careers along by increasing our skills and competence, and by acquiring yet more qualifications. But this also makes us become more threatening, because we then stand out as being much more competent and qualified than everyone else, probably even than our bosses. What we really need to do is to increase our power, assertiveness and visibility, because it is our lack of ability in *these* areas that holds us back.

However, not all women are consistently poor in these areas. Many of the women I interviewed for this book and who are introduced later in this chapter are very successful and have already achieved senior positions. What is striking about all these high achievers is that they are not just highly qualified and good at their job functions. *They are also good at those factors which get successful men to the top!*

They plan their careers (although many of them began to do so only in mid-career), take risks, behave assertively, make themselves visible and face up to challenges. It is not surprising that they have got where they are. Yet they have all managed to make their achievements without sacrificing their femininity and their personal lives. They have all had to work hard and live through tough experiences, yet somehow they have time and energy for whatever it is that for them makes life worth living at a personal level – husbands, boyfriends, children, sport, music, drama, fun, community interests and friends.

Some successful women have got to the top by adopting a male, aggressive model of power and authority. The price they pay for this can be high. A much greater proportion of career women are single, divorced or childless than are their male counterparts. They make sacrifices in their personal lives and they also isolate themselves at work. A male-style aggressive approach to power is very much less attractive and effective when adopted by a woman.

It is far better for a woman to combine being assertive and powerful with being feminine. We do have to toughen up and learn to do what it is that men do to achieve success, but we need to do it in our own way. We must learn to develop some of our own special strengths as women to overcome problems. We are more in touch with our own and other people's feelings and this makes us more approachable and human. We tend to have more stamina, balance and stability. It's a shame to undervalue these strengths in an attempt to model ourselves on our male bosses.

PERSONAL SKILLS

A good proportion of what makes life hard happens inside your own head, and you can do something about it. There are skills and habits you can acquire which will help you to enjoy your work, build good relationships and achieve success. You need to identify those factors which hold you back, and to do something about the ones that are under your control. You must challenge the powerful conditioning which discourages you from facing up to challenges, planning your career and reorganising your life, but you must also recognise that some of this conditioning may be too powerful to counter all at once. A sudden change would be painful if it meant destroying your self-image or losing loved ones. Take one step at a time and you will get there in the end.

Once you begin to develop your personal skills you have a tremendous advantage as a woman. You stand out in the more senior jobs where most of your colleagues are male. Simply because you are a woman you are noticed and remembered, even by other women. So it becomes even easier for you to achieve high visibility.

Our model of a successful woman is one who recognises that she starts out with certain disadvantages, but has gone beyond the stage of complaining about them to that of solving problems. In her attempt to achieve success at work she constantly re-examines the way she lives her whole life. She works out who she is, what she wants out of life, and where she wants to go. She plans her home life as well as her career, understanding that one impinges on the other. She develops the personal skills that help men to succeed but she does so without losing her femininity. She is approachable but firm; a good listener, but clear-thinking and decisive. She is warm, has empathy and stands up for what she thinks is right. She is courageous and risk-taking, but finds a safe shoulder to cry on when she is hurt. When things go wrong she seeks advice and solves her problems. She uses her work skills to help her with her personal life and her female strengths to help her achieve success at work. She knows that it is important to be happy and loved as well as successful. She does what successful men do, but she does more, and she does it differently.

The following chapters develop a complete picture of this model of a successful woman. You will be able to build up a picture of the sort of person you want to become. You will also find practical ways of achieving your goals. En route you will have to recognise the conditioning inside you which holds you back. You will have to decide which changes you can make now, and which are too threatening. By the end you should feel encouraged and clear about where you want to go, and how to get there. But first, let us meet the women who will help to inspire us.

Profiles of success

Success for women, at present, is often associated with making enormous sacrifices. It may mean giving up our personal lives and devoting ourselves single-mindedly to our careers, or for those who are trying to combine a family with a career, success can mean two demanding jobs and having no time for relaxation. This doesn't appeal to me at all. I want to have fun, enjoy my personal life, *and* make achievements. I also don't want to be seen as a dragon, who made it 'at all costs'. Because I think a lot of women feel this way, in this book I want to show that it is possible for a woman to have a career that is enjoyable as well as hard work. And that it *is* possible to get to the top (or high enough) without sacrificing your personal life, and everything else that is important to you as a woman.

To write this book, I interviewed over twenty women. They proved to me that you can make it in a man's world without giving up everything else that makes life rewarding. For my interviews I selected women who seemed to me to be both feminine and successful. By feminine, I don't mean weak, simpering and passive. Feminine to me means being warm, caring and approachable. The women I interviewed combined these qualities with strength and success. Some had families; many did not. Many were in their late thirties or forties, often because they had taken breaks in their careers, and so had taken longer to attain senior jobs. I also interviewed some younger women who had achieved significant success in their twenties, or who seemed to me to be on their way to success.

THE PATHS TO SUCCESS

What interested me about the information I gathered, is how tremendously varied are the paths to success. Some of the women had all the advantages: the right qualifications, helpful parents and good contacts, and they made strong career moves right from the start. But if you're not in this fortunate position, *don't think that means you can't make it*. Several women I interviewed achieved their positions against a background of what initially looked like serious disadvantages. They certainly did not all have degrees or professional qualifications. Many did not have families or contacts who could give them advice and opportunities, and many took long career breaks to have children. Some were single parents. Yet in spite of these problems they had achieved good jobs *and* rewarding personal lives. So take heart, it can be done. Don't assume that top jobs are only for the privileged, or that achieving power and influence at work means that the only one you'll have to talk to at home will be the cat! Learn to have your cake and eat it – as these women did.

Here are profiles of the women I interviewed which give an idea of their characters, their similarities, and show the different routes they followed to achieve success.

Jennifer Rosenberg became enormously successful without the advantage of academic qualifications. Instead of going to university, she elected to have drama training, and this gave her poise and confidence. At her first job, in the post room at Marks and Spencer, she was able to stand out and get noticed. She was chosen to take cheques in to the directors and they soon learnt that she wanted to become a buyer. She was given her chance.

Jennifer has always planned her career and looked ahead two or three years. So when she got to the top as a buyer she became frustrated as she could see no obvious future. Her first marriage had ended in divorce, and her second husband – a supplier to

Marks and Spencer – suggested she set up her own company. She was open with Marks and Spencer, and explained her situation and what she wanted to do. They realised that by having her as a supplier they would keep her expertise. She set up J & J Fashions, a small clothing company. When her second husband died, the company became her personal lifeline and she decided to expand. When she married her third husband, who owned a textile company, they merged the two firms which gave J & J Fashions a unique position as a supplier in that they produce their own fabric. J & J Fashions is now a multi-million pound company and Jennifer is joint chairman along with her husband. In 1987 she was chosen to be Businesswoman of the Year. She wants to continue the growth of J & J Fashions but to keep control of the company. Jennifer has no children but firmly believes that businesswomen should retain their femininity.

Jennifer is purposeful and clear-thinking but not at all off-putting. Although powerful, elegant, and beautifully dressed, she is also disarmingly friendly and open, which adds a feminine touch to her power, and makes it acceptable and attractive.

Sophie Mirman, the chairwoman of the Sock Shop chain, has also become extremely successful without the advantage of a degree or a professional qualification, though she had useful support from her parents who were in retailing. Like Jennifer Rosenberg, Sophie began her working life at Marks and Spencer – in her case in the typing pool. Marks and Spencer seems to be the breeding ground for a lot of successful people! She was lucky enough to work as a secretary for the chairman, who recognised her potential and encouraged and helped her into management. She did well and was earning a large salary when she was invited to join the Tie Rack venture. She couldn't be sure that she would make a success of this but she believes in taking calculated risks.

Once she had firmly established Tie Rack, she took another risk and set up Sock Shop – the success of which is now legendary. Sophie works very hard, yet her personal life is extremely important to her – she has a husband and a young child. She went back to work just ten days after having her baby, but feels that having a baby is probably easier when you run your own company. She has a full-time live-in nanny and a cook. Even though she works so hard, she manages to find time for friends – most of whom work too, so they have much in common. Sophie is charming, down-to-earth, and emanates quiet confidence and fulfilment. She is not at all 'dragonlike', in spite of her success.

Judy Presnell comes from a poor background but has never let this hold her back; she wanted to do well and realised that exams were the key, so she got a degree and professional qualifications as an actuary. Judy is a bright, ambitious woman with clear career goals. She became the youngest ever department manager at the Prudential Assurance, a feat which she achieved at thirty.

She did not then just sit back and relax; she made her further career expectations clear to everyone, without being pushy or aggressive. Four years later she was promoted again and is now in charge of three departments and eighty staff.

Judy is married and has no children. Her particular combination of clear-sightedness, firmness, determination, charm and approachability make her stand out. I first met her on a management course I was running, and I think she will go far.

Aileen Egan went to secretarial college after school and then took her first job at Woolworth. She hated this and decided to spend the rest of her working life doing something she really liked. She was interested in flying, so decided to become an air hostess. (In Ireland, in the 1960s it was unheard of for a woman to study science at university, so her love of aviation and technology could only be indirectly satisfied, in this way.)

Aileen married and had two boys but carried on with her work until her youngest child was four years old. At this point another woman might have retired or taken a long career break, but Aileen took a teacher's training course instead. Then she set up a catering business and taught catering at evening classes. After five years she decided to go back to her first love, aviation. But she was determined to become a manager rather than work as a secretary and spent two years finding out about the aviation industry by working at the local airfield and learning to fly. She then got a job in general management with an aviation company, and gained more experience by doing consultancy work and taking a job as a marketing manager with British Telecom, marketing its products in the aviation world.

Aileen then realised she needed some academic qualifications to increase her credibility in this world of high technology. She is just finishing her MBA at Henley Management College, meanwhile having used her MBA projects both to make herself a leading European expert in the aviation business and to discover where the best job opportunities lie.

Aileen is remarkable because she has chosen a career in what looks like a very male world. Yet she is no male clone. She is a bright, lively, charming woman who looks much younger than her years, she dresses well, in clothes that are both smart and feminine. She is deeply committed to her career, yet also very involved with her husband, children and friends.

Linda Agran is someone who made it after being told she hadn't a chance. When she left school at fourteen her headmistress told her parents that she was stupid, and recommended that she learn to type as the only possible way of earning her keep. Linda says that this boot up her bum has stayed with her ever since.

Linda did start her working life as a typist, but was lured into working for a theatrical agency when she was seventeen by the hope that she would meet and marry a film star. She didn't marry a star, but went one better, by becoming a star herself! Linda loved this job and has stayed in the industry ever since. By making the most of her secretarial and assistant jobs, she got noticed, and promoted – regularly.

Linda's first management job was as Director of Development at Euston Films, a subsidiary of Thames Television. She was responsible for TV serials like *Minder, Widows* and *Ace of Spades*, and for TV films like *Knowledge* and *Charlie Muffin*. Linda's approach to management is to lead from the front: first in and last to leave. She feels that women have more of a gift for management than men because they are better at non-confrontational leadership and at saving face.

Linda lost this job in a political battle with a colleague, which was a terrible blow, but was soon back on her feet in a job at London Weekend Television. There, she rose to be Deputy Controller of Drama at LWT and is now about to start a completely new job as Head of Production at Faravision UK, a company that produces feature films, TV films, TV drama and documentaries.

Linda is an excellent model of female power. To her, being

feminine is certainly not about being pretty, wearing frilly clothes or acting helpless. It is about being herself, which means being an open, flamboyant and funny woman and not being proud, arrogant or aloof. She is not married, but she has a very good, stable relationship. She has never had children but loves other people's.

Angela Moxam is an example of someone who had a career break and then went back to a more senior position than the one she held before. Angela has a degree and post-graduate qualifications in personnel. She met her husband in her first job at Unilever Research and went with him when his work took him to America. She was not able to work for the first two years she was in America because she did not have a work permit and found this very depressing. Eventually however, she was able to do some freelance training for General Electric. By the time she came back to England, where she and her husband divorced, she had three children.

Angela felt she now *had* to get a good job to support herself and her children, and applied for quite a senior job with BIM as Head of Management Development Activities. She managed to convince her interviewers that her experience of managing a family and acting as hostess for her husband, combined with her previous work experience, made her very suitable for the job. This is a case of someone being positive about her role as a wife and mother instead of seeing it as wasted time.

Angela took the job, even though it meant working away from home. She experiences pressure because of her work and home responsibilities, but says that this pressure is not all negative. She is proud that she can earn enough to keep herself and the children, and this ability has increased her confidence. She feels more in control than she did before, and is not always looking out for a 'Prince Charming' to rescue her because she is now self-reliant. Though she would be pleased to meet someone whom she wanted to marry, it is not essential to her happiness.

Angela looks what she is: senior, responsible and decisive. Yet she also exudes a warmth and helpfulness which makes her feminine as well as powerful. She has not been hardened by the problems of being a single parent and a career woman.

Annabel Croft is the youngest person I interviewed. Although only twenty-two, she has had a very demanding career. At fifteen, when she was the number one junior girl tennis player in England, she decided to go on the international tennis circuit. Even though she was Britain's junior champion she started her international career as a nobody without even a computer ranking. For three years she played in every city in the USA, trying to qualify for the big tournaments. At first, she didn't win many matches and felt that no one cared about her, but this experience made her mentally tough and she grew up very quickly. She determined not to give up, because she knew she had the talent.

Eventually she did get up to the top twenties in the world, and became the number one in Britain. But Annabel now feels that at this stage she tried to move on too quickly. Under the pressure, she started to lose matches and finally gave up her career as a competitive tennis player because she no longer enjoyed the game. Yet she is neither hardened nor embittered by the particularly difficult and competitive time she had as a teenager. It taught her a lot about facing up to challenges, doing frightening things and coping with both success and disappointment. She is pleasant, friendly and open, and feminine in both her looks and behaviour. Annabel is now using her hard won experience of performing in front of an audience in a promising new career as a television presenter, having taken over from Anneka Rice as the presenter on the Treasure Hunt programme.

Jean Denton is a freelance director of the public relations company Burston Marsteller, the deputy chairman of the Black Country Development Corporation and a non-executive director of British Nuclear Fuels and the Ordnance Survey. Jean is a competitive person and started her career as a racing driver, a 'sit-down' sport which she chose because she suffered from kidney disease. Often the only woman in a race, she made good contacts and joined the Huxford Group, motor traders, as a market executive and became Marketing Director. She was headhunted by Heron as Marketing Executive, then became Managing Director. Later, she became the Director of External Affairs of the Austin Rover Group.

She wanted to be best at everything she did. She went to a mixed school and felt she had to prove to the world that educating her had been the right thing to do. She didn't have a structured career but believes that the varied experience she gained better qualified her for general management. She thinks she was fortunate to marry someone who was happy for her to go off and do motor racing and work as a manager. Jean considers that in your twenties and early thirties the person you are married to is critical, because that is the time when you are laying the foundation for your career, and if you miss out on the big push at that stage you don't gain the experience you need for getting to the top.

Though Jean and her husband are now divorced she still feels he was a wonderful person. She has not remarried and has no children.

Jean is very busy, yet generous with her time when it comes to helping other women. She is clearly a person of high status, yet she combines her power with a down-to-earth style, openness and wit that is both feminine and very attractive.

Jennifer Haigh worked her way up to board level through jobs as project manager, sales manager, corporate development and general manager. As a result of this broad experience she got a job as Personnel Director of Trebor Limited, the confectionery manufacturer. Now she has moved out of manufacturing and is the Director of Personnel and Administration at British Satellite Broadcasting Ltd.

Jennifer has risen to the top because she works hard and has always been willing to take on new and different types of jobs to build up her experience; she has inner confidence and a belief in herself which saves her from being frightened. Also, she never assumes she knows everything, but calls in experts when she needs them.

Jennifer is not married, but feels that support systems are very important. She employs a home help to do her cleaning and ironing so that she can have more time to relax. Her friends are very important to her. They all work and give each other emotional support. Now in her thirties, Jennifer realises that work alone isn't enough, and is seeking a balance in her life. She is sure of herself and decisive, but also very feminine, warm and friendly.

Esther Denham is recently retired, but she was one of the leading veterinary surgeons in the country and established an excellent animal hospital in Welwyn, Hertfordshire. Esther had wanted to be a vet since the age of five, although her parents had wanted her to be a doctor because that was judged to be a more respectable profession in those days. But they were finally persuaded when, at fourteen, she unflinchingly pulled a needle out of her dog's throat and saved its life.

Esther finished school and joined a veterinary practice on the Isle of Wight. She would have liked to do research but, in order to get a grant (this was 1948), the Ministry of Agriculture and Foods wanted her to promise not to marry for seven years – three while she was at the university and four years working afterwards. These conditions did not fit in with her plans. She wanted a career, marriage and children. She chose her husband, Peter, because, apart from other sterling qualities, he didn't mind her working. They had four children, and Esther took less and less time off from work with each. They are now grown up and successful themselves – and continue to have a close relationship with their mother.

Carey Labovitch started *Blitz* magazine in 1980 when she was studying modern languages at Oxford. She produced the magazine on her bedroom floor. *Blitz* is a life-style magazine for men and women, and it found a gap in the market. After the second issue, Carey realised it had big implications for the future. This was confirmed when the third issue won the Guardian Best Graphics Award.

Carey managed the magazine at first by carrying out all the publishing tasks herself and by getting very good writers and graphic artists to contribute free of charge because they were impressed by the magazine and wanted to support it. She achieved national distribution for *Blitz* while still at university. She feels she took a lot of risks and had a lot of luck.

She built up a publishing company with several magazines, all of which are trendsetters in the publishing world. The company won the BBC Enterprise Award for Small Businesses in 1985 and Carey was the youngest person ever to do so. She is now Managing Director of the Cadogan Press Group which she owns with her partner Simon Tesler. She feels she sacrificed her youth to establish *Blitz* but is very pleased with her achievements. Carey is a shy but pleasant, pretty young woman. Still in her twenties, she is clearly at the top of her field and has made enormous achievements in a very short time, yet she is not at all overwhelming or arrogant.

Elise Smith is also at board director level in publishing, as Managing Director of Becket Publications Ltd – a company which she helped to found a few years ago in the mid 1980s. She publishes *Becket's Directory* which is a who's who of people in the City. Elise, who was born and raised in the United States, has a husband and two children, and has managed to combine a varied and interesting career with motherhood.

Her first profession was as a clinical audiologist (diagnosing hearing difficulties). Then she went to law school, after which she worked for Amnesty International and edited a book on torture. She then set up a needlepoint business and was invited to run Needle Art House, a subsidiary of Johnson Wax. Before founding Becket Publications, she worked for the SDP for five years as fund raiser and editor of their magazine.

Her activities have been very diverse and a lot of fun and she has also had time for her family. Though, in Elise's own words her career has been 'not one I would have had, had I been the main breadwinner', the variety has given her wide experience, and she is in a senior position now. She combines her power, openness, and helpfulness with humour, often directed at herself.

Kirsty Ross is the director of her own consultancy company, called Improving Business Performance. She is married with step-children, but has none of her own. Kirsty is adopted and, although very much loved by her adopted parents, wanted to be independent and successful. Her father encouraged her spirit of independence. He said, 'Women's emancipation comes with their financial independence, so get yourself a degree and it will never come amiss.' Kirsty got herself two degrees and is now Dr Kirsty Ross.

When Kirsty bought her first house her father turned up with a bag of tools and said, 'You've got to get to be handy with these.' She again took his advice, and became a very practical woman. Her mother didn't feel quite the same about her independence and when Kirsty finally walked up the aisle at thirty-five, said, 'Oh good, you'll be able to stop working now!' Of course Kirsty didn't stop.

Her consultancy is successful and expanding and she has recently opened an office in the City. Kirsty is a very clever and powerful woman. She is also large and aware that her size adds to her power. Yet in no way does either her size or power detract from her femininity. She is a loving, friendly person, and very funny.

Fiona Price is also a director of her own company. She is not yet thirty, but has a thriving business in financial advice and planning which she established at twenty-three when she left university. She decided that she could do only two things well, so in her twenties she concentrated on work and sport. Now she is trying to get a better balance in her life and would like a stable relationship and family. She is recruiting other financial experts to help in her business in order to reduce the pressure on her time a little.

Fiona is a powerhouse of a person, competitive in sport as well as in business. Yet her interest in other people shows through and makes her approachable and feminine.

Jacky Woodhouse is communications manager of the Home Service at the Prudential Assurance. She has a husband and two sons. She is famous in this traditionally male company for continuing to work *and* to keep moving upwards after having children.

It never occurred to Jacky that she couldn't combine a career with motherhood. Both her mother and sister run their own businesses. She feels that her children have not lost out in any way through her continuing with a full-time job. In fact, she thinks that the fact that she is away on weekdays has given them a chance to develop as individuals. She is great fun, has a strong personality and her management style is open and encouraging.

Elisabeth Kershaw is associate publisher of *Harpers and Queen*, one of the best-established of the glossy, high quality women's magazines. All the day-to-day decisions concerned with the magazine's production are hers. She is a dynamic person and a keen sportswoman in a world where dynamism and energy are very important.

Elisabeth thinks that being a woman is of great benefit to her in her job. She uses her charm in the largely male world she deals with and finds that this reduces the threat she poses. However, she says 'When a man is being charming it can make him look like a creep!' She feels that she is not competing with men, just with whoever is on the job market – they could be zebras, as far as she is concerned! She knows how to use her advantages and her skills, and she doesn't stab people in the back. Elizabeth is not married.

Some of the women I interviewed had good jobs at middle management or professional level. They were still in their twenties or early thirties and seemed to be heading for outstanding careers.

Avril Hammil works in Eurobond sales with the manufacturers, Hanover Securities; before that she was a marketing manager at British Telecom. She wants to gain experience in a number of different areas so that she can eventually get a job at managing director level. Avril's parents were working-class and they didn't pressurise her or give her any guidance or direction about her career. Nevertheless, she went to university and studied science.

After her first job at Unilever, which she didn't like, she landed a job selling pharmaceuticals, and loved it. She was promoted because her sales were good and she was excellent at planning and organising.

Avril is always looking ahead to the future. She is bright and dynamic, yet friendly and chatty and has the knack of making you feel as if you are important in her eyes when you talk.

Anne Millet is an Account Director at Option One to Eleven, a public relations company. When she started her first job at twenty-one for a marketing consultancy company called Marketing Solutions she used to wonder how on earth she could be credible enough to advise marketing directors who were twenty years her senior. It took her three years to begin to feel comfortable in her role, and she was promoted to account director and grew in stature and confidence. Still in her twenties, she now feels that her age is less of an issue.

Anne was clear from the start that she wanted a career and chose jobs that weren't dead ends. She is now married and hopes to combine being successful at work with a happy personal life –

including children. She is very pretty and charming as well as determined, ambitious and able to work very hard.

Pauline Buchanan Black is the Director of the London Housing Association's Training Scheme where she is in charge of ten full-time staff and two hundred consultants. Pauline got married at twenty, when she was still at art school and spent a year living on her husband's student grant and didn't work. This didn't seem wrong or out of order to her, but *now* she couldn't imagine not working.

She began doing voluntary work which eventually became a full-time career. While still in her twenties she did two risky things: she ended her first marriage which was comfortable but unrewarding, and she also left Liverpool for London, resigning from her job on Merseyside where she was well known in the voluntary sector and had become a local media personality. She was a big fish in a little sea, but with nowhere further to go, so she went to London to take up a hard, challenging job, also in the voluntary sector, and for a time she regretted her decision. She left this job and started flying hot air balloons! This didn't last too long, as it was seasonal, so she worked as a consultant until she got her present job.

She lives with her boyfriend and they have a baby. Pauline impresses you the minute she walks into a room as being a person in charge of herself and of the situation. She combines her leadership ability with being able to listen and empathise.

June Campbell, a vivacious redhead, is a product manager at British Telecom where she has been since she graduated from university. Career planning never featured in her thinking and she graduated with no clear idea of what to do and just went after anything that looked interesting. She initially applied for the job to pay off an overdraft and to buy herself a flat! But she likes it and was promoted after three years, because she was in the right place at the right time and showed that she was willing to work and travel.

She now looks at things more clinically: she wants to continue to be promoted and knows what to do to make it more likely. She is aware of the job opportunities both outside and within the company, and is determined to make a success of her career.

Fiona MacMillan and **Susan Port** are executive search and recruitment consultants with the PA consulting group and gave me a lot of help in researching the chapter on interviewing. They are both young, dynamic and very professional, but also warm, funny and friendly. They are both married, but have no children.

Fiona was awarded a law degree by Aberdeen University, then spent several years with Peat Marwick McLintock doing legal and accountancy work on liquidations and receivership. She next joined a small accountancy recruitment firm and from there she went to PA to set up an accountancy recruitment division and was promoted to become a headhunter specialising in financial jobs.

Susan Port has a degree in psychology from University College, London University. Her first job was in British Home Stores as a management trainee. She then joined a trade organisation providing information for companies wanting to send staff abroad. She joined PA after that, first as an executive search researcher, then as a recruitment consultant, and is now one of their headhunters.

Marianne Bruce is an artist. Her first job, which she started as a teenager, was as a dancer with the Ballet Rambert. The discipline which she learnt in that profession has helped her to stick with her art, in spite of having three children. She had to give up dancing when she had her first child, and when her first two children were still very young she decided to study art. Marianne was talented and determined. She went to the local art college, and turned a room in her house into a studio. She experienced difficulties because she had to combine her profession with motherhood, and her husband's job often took him away from home. In her late thirties she went to university.

Marianne continues to have a studio in her house and paints at every possible opportunity. She exhibits her work regularly. She has a dancer's poise and clear, thoughtful eyes, and is both very determined and very womanly.

Having given you a brief outline of these women's careers and aspirations, I will be using their experience to illustrate points in every chapter. Many of their quotes will be anonymous, to protect the innocent – and the guilty! I would like to thank them all for their fascinating tales and their helpfulness.

2
Female power

People at the top know how to use power and authority (as do people on the way to the top), but for women seeking success and senior jobs this can be a major problem. Powerful positions are won by personally powerful people and those without this quality are unlikely to find themselves up there. But, in our society, a majority of women still grow up accepting that men are powerful and woman are not. This conditioning starts early – within the family and is reinforced by school and the media. Little girls can be organising and assertive in ways that are quite acceptable – it seems to come naturally to them – yet at puberty they often discard this behaviour in favour of a more acquiescent, feminine style, whereas aggression, risk-taking and leadership actively continue among boys.

PERSONAL POWER
The ability to behave in a powerful way is vital in senior jobs. In all my years as a consultant I never met anyone with a top job in any organisation, large or small, who did not behave in a powerful, authoritative way. There seems to be no place at these top, decision-making levels for people who are acquiescent,

unassertive or lacking in confidence. I have met several senior people who lack one or two of the other qualities that tend to go with success; for example I know some senior people who are very aggressive, and many who are appalling at meetings. Sometimes they are powerful in a negative, threatening way, which is a form of power I caution women against using. I also know some top managers in large bureaucratic organisations who behave cautiously and don't like taking risks. But whatever qualities they may lack, they are all powerful in one way or another. Even people working for themselves need to become powerful in their dealings with the sometimes difficult and demanding world outside – the world of customers, clients and suppliers.

What I mean when I use the term 'power', is the ability to get things to happen for you, to get others to behave in a particular way or to carry out certain actions. There are, however, different forms of power which can be acquired through your position in the hierarchy or through your skill or expertise. All forms of power can be used either positively to reward or negatively to harm.

Reward power is the ability to give a person something they want or to take away something they find negative. So if you give someone a pay increase or transfer them out of a job they don't like you are using your reward power.

Coercive power is the ability to punish someone with something they find negative or to remove a reward. An example of this, is refusing to allow your assistant to take on a desirable project because her report writing is still too poor.

Legitimate power means using your position or responsibilities to get people to accept your influence and do what you want them to do – when you delegate work, for example.

Referent power comes when people want to identify with you or be like you. Successful people often find that others in their field want to be associated with them or use them as role models.

Expert power is gained by having some special skill. So accountants, lawyers, computer specialists and artists can use skills which other people don't have, to influence them.

Information power comes as a result of having knowledge or information which is of use to other people. If you are up-to-date on the latest developments in your field, for example, this knowledge will make you powerful in your contact with people who need it but haven't got it.

POSITIVE POWER

Power also comes from the way a person behaves, and this is linked with how they feel about themselves. This is called *positive personal power* and it comes from maturity, security in one's relationships, lack of need to gain from others and confidence in one's impulses. These people are strong because they trust themselves. Their behaviour is not dominated by a need to conform, to be liked, to rebel, to lead, or manipulate others. They are relatively autonomous and decisive, and have a strong sense of responsibility. It is this personal power, that comes from within, that is so important. Without this inner strength, as well as the courage to use their authority, it is difficult for people of *either* sex to get to the top.

NEGATIVE POWER

This form of power is exercised by people who are compensating for psychological problems. These people feel vulnerable for some reason and manipulate and take power from others in order to protect themselves. They are often overbearing, intrusive and arrogant and it is not surprising that women who are on the receiving end of such power are put off by it, and don't want to become powerful themselves.

In my own career as a management consultant, I have had several encounters with people using negative personal power and I always find it threatening. I remember meeting a senior woman in a large company who disagreed strongly with a project her boss had invited me to carry out. This woman used all the negative power she could summon to discourage me. She condemned my proposals as being out of line with the company culture, and misconceived. She never smiled once in an hour-long meeting but looked at me with cold, angry eyes. She frequently interrupted when I was speaking and, when I tried to get her to discuss her disagreements objectively, simply restated them in a way that showed she had no intention of changing her mind.

However, I went ahead with the project and it proved very successful. The woman who had predicted failure was the first to congratulate me and admit that she had been wrong. Yet the experience of our first encounter had shaken me. I had to gather up all my resources of courage to carry on with the project, even though I knew I was right.

Many women back away from using power because they have been put off by such negatively-powerful people. Women, who tend to have strong needs to be liked, do not want to model themselves on such people. Early lessons about power are learnt in the family, where the first powerful role in a woman's life is often her father. He need not be arrogant and overbearing, but in a traditional family where he is the main breadwinner, she cannot help noticing when his relative power has a negative effect on her mother. The traditional mother, acting as a support to her husband, may be seen as having a life of menial chores, restricted freedom and underused talents. The power and freedom which her father has, through going out to work and having his domestic needs catered for, may be seen as being selfish, and thereby denying her mother her rights. A young girl observing this may draw the conclusion that being powerful means being selfish; that acting for oneself means depriving others.

SOCIAL CONDITIONING
Society withholds social power from women. Even in families where enlightened parents try to raise their daughters like their sons, the message gets through via schools, friends and the media.

The social image of powerful women is often a terrifying one. They are equated with destruction or with emasculated men, or pilloried as lesbians. Why should this be? Throughout history, men have been in awe of women's capacity to give life. Frightened – and envious – of this power, they have tried to assuage their anxiety by creating a variety of myths about powerful women. There is the destructiveness of Helen of Troy, the Sirens luring men to their death, Medusa, Eve tempting Adam, and woman as the insatiable whore. A popular subject for current television drama is the suffering of husbands married to insensitive, ambitious career women. No wonder many women have second thoughts about 'stepping out of line' and using power.

Not only do men see powerful women as a threat, but women themselves can feel threatened by the thought of being powerful. The traditional definition of femininity is to be submissive, tender and soft. The negative attributes associated with femininity are being weak, over-emotional, too compassionate, frivolous, passive, submissive, inexpert and suffocatingly supportive. These are all the qualities of a loser in any game – except the game of winning a man's love – and probably there as well, except in romantic fiction!

A book recently published, which guarantees that its readers would get themselves a husband within a year, gives this advice: 'Talk less about yourself; learn to ask a man lots of questions about himself, and listen enthusiastically to the answers.' This is traditional feminine behaviour, spelt out in fine detail.

Winning a man's love has been the primary goal of women throughout history. Brought up to deny our own power and to seek power and status through the man we marry, we are naturally reluctant to discard feminine attributes. They were, after all, traditionally a woman's only sure route to success – via a man – until as recently as the early 1900s. Women had no autonomy or civil rights, and were truly dependent upon men. They could not vote and had to give over their property to their husbands.

Women have made much progress over their civil and property rights in this century, but we can't throw away the past without a thought. And it is an undeniable fact that men *still* effectively hold the reins of power.

Even young women who have been brought up to see themselves as equal to men are ambivalent over the issue of power. All of my interviewees, whatever their age, expressed *some* problems to do with wielding power, even though many of them liked to be, or wanted to be, powerful.

PERSONAL DILEMMAS
So, a woman poised on the threshold of a promising career which could catapult her into the power élite, is faced with a great dilemma. If she grasps these opportunities and enjoys the success and fulfilment which she hopes for, will she miss out on getting a good man to love her and provide her with children?

If she becomes a successful, powerful businesswoman, will she find her life empty of all the other things she needs? Women risk social isolation by becoming too powerful. Some men react against a woman's attempts to become powerful in her own right. How often have we heard the crude statement, 'What she needs is a man'? Power can isolate a woman from her male colleagues and potential lovers, and it can also isolate her from other women who feel threatened, jealous or betrayed.

I know several women who find themselves in this position. One finds herself in her middle thirties with a good job, a powerful position and a high income but with a void in her life when it comes to personal relationships. She is unhappy and feels as if she has failed, in spite of having an excellent career. She would dearly like to have a husband, and possibly children, to give her life more balance. This woman has also isolated herself at work from some of her colleagues because of her blunt, slightly aggressive form of power. She is neither happy in her personal life nor her work life, and is not reaping any emotional rewards from her achievements.

Men can be ambivalent about female power. On the one hand, they find it frightening and run away from it or they try to denigrate powerful women by trivialising the work that they do. This can be a difficulty for women who are serious about their jobs but also want rewarding personal relationships with men. On the other hand, some men find powerful women attractive. Here are quotes from thee men who have thought it over very carefully:

If you know someone is powerful and successful, then you're automatically interested in them. The trouble with powerful people – men and women – is that they often put you off by talking too much and being overbearing. So when a successful woman does this she is not attractive. However, when she combines her power (which makes her interesting) with knowing her own mind and being warm and interested in me and what I have to say, then she can be very attractive. I certainly don't like helpless women.

It's not that power and achievement in a woman are attractive *per se*. I feel these things are neutral, but that they don't necessarily *detract* from attractiveness. I find a woman sexually attractive if she exhibits enough character to make me feel as if she will be uninhibited, not submissive, active and appreciative in bed. Women like this are much more appealing than those who are very soft, feminine and helpless. Now, inasmuch as successful women display this strength of character they will be attractive. And they often are, unless they overdo the power thing and their aggression puts you off.

Successful career women are becoming more acceptable among

my age group (twenties). I don't necessarily look for it, but I don't find it threatening. Power doesn't make a woman less attractive or more attractive. It's not an issue.

So there are men who enjoy being with career women and who value their strengths. Nonetheless, many of the young women I interviewed notice that their economic independence is a threat to their prospective boyfriends.

When they realise that I have a good job, my own house and car and that I can look after myself, some of them back away. I am too much of a challenge to them.

Many of the women interviewed saw power as an area of great difficulty for a career woman.

Men treat you as an equal at college. It's only when you go to work and get better jobs and salaries that you threaten. Power isolates and endangers your personal life. It's the middle phase of your career, when you're really growing, that puts a marriage under pressure. Husbands just don't give the support for women that wives do for men. Power poses problems for single women as well as married women. A man who is interested in you will allow you to break a date twice because of business commitments, but the third time you get struck off the list.

Many women would also find this sort of treatment annoying, but they tend to give their personal relationships a higher priority than men do, so would be less inclined to give up on a promising commitment, even if it is in its early stages. This sort of date-breaking behaviour may also seem slightly more acceptable in a man; indeed, it may increase his desirability by giving him an aura of power and success, even though it causes frustration and disappointment. The wives and girlfriends of successful men have learnt that broken dates are part of the package. Because there are so few senior career women around, men haven't, in general, learnt to expect or cope with the way business commitments can interfere with the personal lives of these women. They will, therefore, look elsewhere rather than suffer this blow to their ego.

THE THREAT OF WOMAN POWER

Not only can a woman's power threaten her personal life, it can also cause problems with her colleagues at work. Most men are accustomed to relating to women as wives, daughters, and secretaries – all people whom they see as less powerful than themselves – and when they encounter female colleagues with equal or more power they find it difficult to adjust. Many men simply do not like being told what to do by a woman. A competent, well-balanced man will adjust, over time, but there are plenty of incompetent or vulnerable men who are very threatened and they often use skilful, if underhand, power-strategies against the women in question. In the interviews I heard several tales of women who had lost out in power struggles with vulnerable, threatened men.

So, women are faced with Catch 22 over the issue of female power. If we don't use power and authority we will not get to the top but if we do use power we risk being seen as aggressive, unfeminine, emasculating and threatening. Because there are few role models of senior, powerful but feminine women, those of us faced with this choice will often back away from becoming truly powerful. This is regrettable, as there are ways round the problem. Here are some quotes from senior women who view tough, powerful behaviour as distasteful, but have all developed feminine, alternative ways of using their authority.

> The reason why I am not powerful and dragonlike is because I once had a male dragon for a boss. I would hate to be so unapproachable, so I don't put myself on a pedestal. I prefer to win people's confidence and co-operation by knowing their strengths and weaknesses.

> I have to behave in a powerful way when I am consulting with senior people, otherwise I would have no credibility. Yet I know I tread on a tightrope: too much power and I will seem domineering; too little power and I will seem weak and indecisive. I use everything I've got: powerful behaviour, telling people what I think, confronting them when I need to, and power dressing, but I still try to look and behave like a woman, not a man. All of this needs to be combined with what I consider to be the feminine qualities of empathy, warmth and understanding, without which

my direct and powerful behaviour would make me seem like a dragon.

Men don't want a woman around them who uses tough behaviour, although they do accept firmness. I think a woman should guard against using a man's style of leadership. It's very important not to lose your feminity. For example, I believe in talking things through with people before acting because if I don't, I may get it wrong. I think people find this more acceptable.

I'm not wild about being powerful in the way that men are powerful. The male ego is quite fragile. They're much more conscious of power and status than women are. Yet I haven't got a problem in telling people what to do. I usually persuade rather than tell. People prefer to do things because they understand rather than because they are told what to do.

So far in this chapter it must seem as if women stand little chance of getting to the top because of the dilemmas over the use of power. However, the threat of female power is less about the use of power *per se*, but more about women using male, aggressive, macho models of power. We can use power without losing lovers, friends and allies at work, but we must use a form of power which does not deny our femininity.

The way through the dilemma also involves redefining femininity, away from the traditional negative view, towards a more positive one in line with the needs of successful women in the late 1980s and 1990s. We can face all sorts of difficulties in our efforts to get it right:

In my early days as a manager I struggled with the problem of being authoritative while holding on to my femininity. It wasn't difficult for me to be independent and assertive, as I had always been that way inclined, but the femininity bit I got completely wrong. My idea of being feminine was looking sexy, frilly and provocative. I wore short, tight skirts and pastel colours with frills and bows. My clothes were expensive and well made, but they were quite inappropriate. I found it difficult to get people to take me seriously. My achievements and competence were acknowledged, but I was never able to be influential.

I see so many female yuppies today getting the power thing wrong. They have learnt how to power dress in a feminine way by using colour and jewellery with their designer suits, but their behaviour is terribly male and aggressive. They are self confident and energetic, but somehow brash and hard. The warm, female side seems to be missing, more so in fact than in many men! Their attempts to be feminine are only superficial.

Developing a positive female style of power is the answer to a career woman's growth, but clearly it is not easy. First, you have to turn inwards, and confront those deep-seated attitudes towards power which may be holding you back from acquiring or using it. Then you need to cultivate a style which combines the 'male' strengths of independence and assertion with the 'female' strengths of nurturing and collaboration. Using power effectively demands highly-skilled behaviour. Training courses will help with the development of these skills, but first you must be clear about what sort of power it is you are trying to use.

PATRISM AND MATRISM
Psychologists have identified two fundamentally different approaches to power which they call 'Patrism' and 'Matrism'.

● *Patrism* is the traditionally male form of leadership: tough (as opposed to radical and tender) and based on a belief in order, discipline and respect for authority. It values self-control and rational behaviour and makes a strong distinction between male and female behaviour. It puts faith in age and experience rather than youth.[6] Men wielding this form of power use people and ignore their needs. They make occasional grand gestures but don't really think about people's personal needs and problems:

I have a client who makes 'grand gestures'. He has a subordinate who is under terrible pressure, so much so that he is drinking too much and beginning to make poor decisions at work. What this person needs is help in reducing the pressure, and support from his boss. Instead of that, the boss sends him on a holiday to the Caribbean. Great, but he comes right back to the pressure and soon everything is as bad as it was before.

The quickest way to power is the old, traditional way – ignore people's needs and use them.

● *Matrism*, on the other hand, is a form of leadership that prefers discussion to just giving orders. It is optimistic about the future, believes in openness and makes little distinction between the sexes. It relies on expertise rather than experience, and values youth and imagination rather than age.[6]

It would be a gross over-simplification to say that all powerful men use patrism and all powerful women use matrism. Many pioneering business women in tough environments have developed extreme forms of patrism, and see it as their only means of survival. And conversely, although most men do still use patrism, there is a noticeable swing, in both Britain and the USA, towards matrism. There is a growing sense amongst top-level managers that in order to achieve significant change they must pay attention to the needs of their people:

I feel that the only route to success for leaders is to nurture and facilitate rather than to police. Women tend to lead from the front and to delegate better. Women managers' secretaries have more power than those of men managers. Women have to be more flexible and this is an advantage when it comes to managing change. They are often better at communicating because they're less structured and rigid. Women's style of leadership is different, but it's not *wrong*. In fact it brings many advantages.

There is a price to be paid when macho aggressive leaders favour patrism, and it is paid personally by the men and women using it – as well as by their organisations. This male model of leadership and power is to show outward strengths, to cover over weaknesses and to hide inner anxieties. You don't own up when you don't know; you pretend you do know and bluff your way through. You stay tough and don't talk about how it feels. This leads to a feeling of isolation because you can't share your feelings, so you think it's just you suffering from anxiety, insecurity and inner conflicts. The myth is that, in order to get on, you must compete with everyone.

Patrism, with its belief in order and discipline, is a form of leadership and power that does not cope easily with change and uncertainty. These leaders, when faced with uncertainty, polarise problems into black or white, react negatively rather than take the initiative, flare up, withdraw, work harder and longer and escape into drinking bouts or other forms of harmful behaviour. Eventually they may break down. This is hardly a healthy model for women to imitate. For a woman to be successful, therefore, she must develop her own positive form of power. And in order to do that she must re-examine her definitions of femininity; if these are so traditional that they conflict with the development of her power, she will find it hard to progress. On the other hand, sensing this conflict between femininity and power she may choose power and deny her femininity. Then she risks alienating both her male and female colleagues, damaging her personal life, and adopting a style of leadership which is unprogressive.

As already stated, femininity traditionally meant passivity, weakness, delicacy and girlishness. It placed stress on appearance and presentation and implied coyness, coquettishness, and strategies (feminine wiles). Now femininity is being redefined, with emphasis on the ability to show tenderness, sensitivity and nurturance. This definition does not conflict with being powerful. Women are learning that they can be tender and giving as well as being strong and powerful.

CARING AND GIVING
Many of the senior women whom I interviewed have developed a successful style of leadership that combines positive personal power with caring about other people. Thus they can remain true to themselves without alienating others. They have also found that while using power is not without its problems, it also brings advantages:

> Most of your power comes from inside of you. Real power is the ability to influence things from your personality, what you know about the organisation and your ability to use strategy. If your use of power is consistent with what you believe in, then you can feel OK about it and include caring for others. Then being powerful is nice.

> I enjoy having power. I like people to know I have entered a room.

The upsides of power are greater than the downsides. You have more choice and independence. You tend to be doing what you choose to do. The confidence of age and ability takes time to acquire, but once you've got it, it's good. Now that I am in a powerful position I feel I don't mind if other people don't like what I do. I am clear about my objectives and I try to achieve them if *I* think they're right.

Being powerful is thrilling. Sure, it brings responsibilities and some sacrifices, but what people who aren't powerful don't realise is that it brings fun and excitement. It's lovely to feel that you are in charge of your own destiny, that you have the freedom to make important decisions, and that you actually have some choice about how you live your life. It's much less frustrating than being powerless. To me the greatest advantage is that powerful people get lots of attention. To a woman getting older, being powerful is an excellent alternative to youthful good looks as a way of being in the centre of things. The power that comes through achievement and position is much more effective and long lasting than the power that comes through beauty. And it's not necessarily either/ or. Power can make you very attractive.

So the first step is to use power in a way which is true to your femininity; and will be non-threatening to most people. However, there will be weak or vulnerable men and women who see female power as a threat in whatever form they experience it and to defend themselves they will use negative power strategies against you. You need to be alert to these dangers and have your own power defence strategies ready for such encounters.

One interviewee provided an illuminating example of negative power used against a competent senior woman.

At my last job my boss was not the brightest of people. I picked up on a number of areas that he was not good at. When he saw that I was more competent than he was, he actively obstructed me. In order to carry out an important project it was necessary for me to attend a particular training course. The day before the course my boss said, 'I don't want you to go on that course.' He was clearly blocking my progress, so I persisted. He simply said, 'I'm the boss and I don't want you to go.' I left the room to consider my options.

I decided not to confront him with his unreasonable, blocking behaviour and found a way of attending another, slightly later course.

In the long term I lost out. Even though I could see he was obstructing me because I threatened him by showing up his inadequacies, I did nothing strategic to protect myself. Two months later he made me redundant. He had set up the process for this immediately after the training course incident. He chose a time when his boss was out of the country so I had no one to appeal to. I should have seen this coming and taken up the matter with my boss's boss to protect myself in good time.

Another woman had an equally distressing experience.

I didn't realise that I had made an enemy of this man, but I obviously had. He wanted me out of the company so that he could run it on his own. He achieved that because of his friendship with the director of the holding company, and I lost my job.

I felt really bad about it. I couldn't just treat it as a fact of life, all my emotions came into play. I felt I had sacrificed marriage and children and suddenly it wasn't worth it any more. I saw my whole life as a failure. I couldn't go out, couldn't speak to friends. I contemplated legal action but realised I would be the only loser.

I crept away to Portugal on a holiday and, while I was there, someone telephoned and made me a very good job offer. Throwing myself into this new work helped me to recover but the scar has never gone away.

POWER NETWORKS

Another form of power is the indirect power which comes from who you know and who you can influence. Men take the trouble to build informal networks of contacts at work. This gives them greater power and influence and means that they have people they can turn to if they are in trouble. Women also need to increase their power by building these networks. Had the women in the above cases built up a network of senior allies, they may have been able to elicit their help to prevent such harsh treatment.

The first step in building a network of powerful allies is to ask yourself, 'Where do I stand now? Do I spend enough of my time meeting and communicating with powerful people?' One good way of clarifying your present position is to draw a communication map. Put yourself in the middle, then put all the people you communicate with in a circle round you. Draw thick black lines from your central position to the people you communicate with most frequently, and thinner or dotted lines to those you have less contact with. Finally, underline all the powerful people on your map. Then you will see at a glance whether you spend most of your time with powerful or less powerful people.

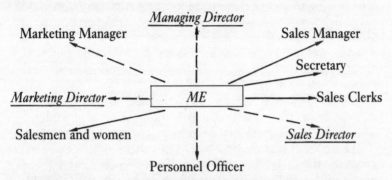

The person in the middle of this example is a senior sales woman who is excellent at her job, very competent and could have a good career, but is she devoting enough time to building powerful allies? Not according to her communication map. She spends most of her time with those at her level or below, and far too little with more senior people.

If you are in this position, work out a strategy for increasing your contacts with more senior people. In some cases, you may simply need to break the comfortable habit of spending time only with junior people. In other cases, the job may not provide enough opportunities for you to interact with senior people, or your boss may block you from speaking to them. Sometimes a transfer to another job will provide better opportunities, or perhaps you could take on a high profile project.

When I joined a management consultancy company I very quickly got to know the other people in my department. They were all either secretaries or other consultants at my level. It was enjoyable having good working relationships and I was happy to spend most of my time with these people. Fortunately, my boss was keen to assist me with my career and did his best to help me to make contact with more senior, influential people in the company. He arranged meetings with them, and got me working on projects in association with them. As a result I became known around the company and this helped me to get an early promotion. It would never have occurred to me to do this of my own accord, and I owed my early career successes to the fact that my boss showed me how to build a power network.

Power strategies are not time-wasting. In order to lead effectively and to progress you have to use power; if you don't your talents will be ignored or under-used. Yet when you become powerful you may find yourself in danger from vulnerable people, and you will need a truly solid power base to protect yourself.

POWER UNDER THREAT

Attacks on powerful women can come from other women, particularly those who see themselves as weak and powerless. A woman who has strong positive personal power is simultaneously the object of emulation and hatred by other women; by her very presence she makes powerless women feel uncomfortable as her achievement makes it difficult for them to say, 'I can't achieve because women face too many obstacles'.

These weaker, threatened women will attack in subtle, indirect ways, trying to inhibit the stronger woman from her leadership by making her feel guilty. They may make her feel she is denying them something they need, or trampling over them. Thus she may hesitate to contradict or chastise when she needs to. Weaker women perceive power as being in limited supply. If one person has it the other cannot. They therefore experience the stronger woman's power as blocking theirs.

Powerful women have to become sensitive to the feelings they generate in other women, and to their power needs. Having power means having more responsibility, and behaving in a sensitive, supportive way in order not to be experienced as threatening by other women. But it is also essential not to let such considerations mute your leadership.

SKILFUL POWER PLAY

Using power effectively is partly a question of having the courage to do so and believing that you can wield it without being unfeminine, but it is also a matter of being strategic and skilful.

One interviewee provided this very good example of the need for strategy and skill in reducing smoking in her department.

> At first I just rushed in like a bull in a china shop and said, 'There is to be no smoking here'. Not only did the smokers get very aggressive, but when I was away they smoked all day. When I moved to manage a new office I used a different strategy. I made it clear that I didn't like smoking and circulated some anti-smoking articles, along with a memo saying I thought smoking was damaging and asking for people's views, particularly smokers. The smokers said they understood the problems and would accept restrictions. Now the office is virtually non-smoking and there is no bad feeling.

Her second strategy was successful because she used her power to make it clear that she thought smoking was undesirable, yet in a way which was non-threatening to the smokers.

This woman also felt that a sense of humour is worth cultivating:

> Humour is very powerful. If you stand up for yourself in a nice, funny way you win through and influence people. However, you've got to be sensitive to when you shouldn't speak up.

Another interviewee felt that a good strategy for using power is to use it openly.

> Usually when I use power openly I'm not challenged. Once I announced at a meeting that I was going to take the chair and did so. Even the man who had previously announced that he planned to chair this meeting accepted my decision

If you exercise your right to use power and authority from the outset, and do so with confidence in a non-threatening way, then by and large other people will accept your authority.

THE AUTHORITY OF POWER

It is also important how other people perceive your power resources. You may have the position to have legitimate power, or the skill to have expert power, but if others don't recognise you as having the position or skill you will not be able to use power. This can often be a problem for women newly promoted into positions of authority who find that the people they come into contact with resist giving that sort of authority to a woman. In these cases, use patience, humour, persistence, confrontation – whatever tactic you judge to be appropriate.

Ironically it is often other women, particularly secretaries, who can give the career woman the most trouble. A secretary might feel that it lowers her status to work for a woman. One of the women I interviewed had a secretary who delayed typing *her* work and always gave preferential treatment to the men in her section. This woman had to use her power openly and take her secretary aside and talk to her about the problem *twice* in order to get a lasting change for the better. This was a case where quiet but firm confrontation was necessary, and also persistence in the face of backsliding.

When you move into a senior position it is important that you are seen to use the power and authority that go with that role. Some people may resist you, but most will be expecting you to use your authority and will be lost and confused if you don't. One woman manager, newly-promoted, found that her staff expected her to behave with authority. 'As soon as I realised that, I made it clear that I would make the final decision, even when I asked people to give me their ideas for solutions.'

Power is probably the biggest single issue that a woman has to grapple with on her way to the top. It is often not seen as an issue while you are on the lower levels of the hierarchy, but as soon as you start to get to levels where you have to use your authority – to say no as well as yes – the issue raises its head. People will then begin both to respect you and to find you threatening – they are responding to your power. You can't avoid it if you want to do well. The answer is to face up to power and learn to use it in a way which is feminine and constructive.

3
Influencing others

Effectiveness at work is about achieving goals and getting things done. We women often lose sight of the fact that it's not enough to be good at our jobs; we must also influence people within our organisations and, even perhaps, in a wider sphere.

It may seem strange at first sight to have one chapter on power and another on influence, since these two words are often used interchangeably. However, there is a difference:

- Power is a resource – it's the *ability* to get things to happen for you.
- Influence is what you achieve by using your power.

There might be two people who are equally powerful because they have equal positions in the company hierarchy, but one may be more influential than the other because she uses her power resources more effectively.

Being influential, as a woman, has several aspects:

- Overcoming the barriers which hold you back from being strategic and political.
- Knowing who to influence and how to go about it.

• Being skilful enough in your behaviour so that people are inclined to pay attention to you and cooperate.
This chapter deals with all of these three aspects.

Company politics

One barrier to women's influence comes from a tendency to be naïve about the informal power network, and from our distaste for getting involved in company politics. One interviewee explained:

> There is a tremendous amount of time-wasting politics in the company. I prefer not to get involved. It's difficult to see anything positive coming out of company politics.

This attitude is common among many career women, and it is one which will hold us back from being influential.

Another barrier is an external one. We are largely excluded from the informal power networks – composed of men – which are already well established in most organisations. Because women are often token, or few in number at senior levels, we don't get included in these informal groups, and this isolation limits our influence.

In these networks, men exchange information about who has the power, about acceptable ways of behaving, about influence strategies and about how to pull strings. Thus they gain access to information, powerful allies and the social contacts they need for support. They may discover, for example, who to approach before a meeting in order to get support for their views. In Chapter 2 we saw how contacts can help to protect you against unfair treatment. These contacts are largely made in the informal networks that men almost instinctively make or join.

Because women are often excluded from these networks they don't perceive the political environment accurately – they don't have access to the information that would explain it to them. Therefore, they may not grasp the importance of the political system as a legitimate way of getting things done, and often become baffled and frustrated by their inability to gain recognition and influence.

When a man joins an organisation the informal network helps him with his apprenticeship. He gets to know people who can assist him in learning about the company's beliefs and attitudes, and he finds out the appropriate methods for getting things done. A woman's apprenticeship will be slower, more painful and less complete because of her lack of access to these networks. As a result, she may develop values and attitudes that are markedly different from those of her male colleagues, reinforcing her difficulties in fitting-in and influencing.

What can a woman do to overcome these barriers? The first step is to recognise informal networking as a legitimate way of getting things done. Competence without the ability to influence and make things happen means wasting a lot of effort. If no one outside your immediate sphere knows of you, then you are of limited value in your field. To be able to contribute fully, you need to be in touch with what's going on, why, and who is doing it.

INFORMAL CONTACTS
Build up your own network of informal contacts as a way of gaining access to information, winning allies and learning the ropes. It is very difficult to get into senior positions and stay there without friends. Your network of allies is as important to your effectiveness as your expertise and qualifications.

I have spent a lot of time watching men build up their informal networks. They are much more inclined than women are to suggest a lunch or a visit to the pub. They also arrange social events outside working hours, which often include spouses, and are excellent occasions for building the friendly relations you need for being considered the next time a big project is in the offing. Men are also often very good at keeping in touch on the telephone, and calling contacts to ask for help or information. At social events where they are meeting new, possibly useful contacts, the skilful ones chat about work and swap information about what they do in a friendly, laid-back way. If it looks as if they can be of use to each other they exchange cards, arrange to meet sometime and then change the subject. In this way they make contacts without becoming bores.

Quite recently my husband arranged a game of tennis with a man he had been working for in a large company. Wives were included, and we played mixed doubles. As a result of chatting about work afterwards, I received a phone call a few weeks later from the personnel department of this company inviting me to tender for some consultancy work. The tennis-playing contact had given my name and a personal recommendation. The end result was a big new client for my business. Several good work opportunities have come to me in this way, and I now make a deliberate effort to increase the amount of informal networking that I do. In the past I had to think of an excuse before I phoned someone or invited them to lunch. Now I do so to keep in touch. I've learnt that you don't need an excuse. If you build up a good relationship informally it increases trust, and with it the likelihood that they will prefer to put opportunities your way.

WHAT TO DO ABOUT MALE NETWORKS

Even knowing that informal networking is useful, you may still find it difficult to move forward because of the predominantly male nature of most of these networks. This is something you have to be creative and clever about. If you try to join in on beer and dirty joke sessions, behave like one of the boys and deny your femininity – it doesn't work. Men don't like macho, unfeminine women. You will have to find ways of making friends, and joining male groups without denying your femaleness. Look for compromises and use your judgement about acceptable behaviour. You can get a lot of help from other women in the same predicament by joining appropriate women's networks. It also helps to find someone (male or female) within your organisation who will act as your mentor and give you advice on these delicate situations.

When building or joining informal networks, look for common ground. Try to chat about interests in common – cars, music, sport, travel, whatever this may be. You don't have to drink yourself silly in a pub with male colleagues, but you may be able to make friends through playing squash or going to concerts.

Be alert and use opportunities. If you are excluded from some of the all-male events then compensate in other ways, by taking time out to chat or arranging a quick drink or lunch on your own terms.

BUILD RELATIONSHIPS TO WIN ALLIES

An attitude which many women have, and which makes it difficult to build informal networks, is that, 'my home life is quite separate from my working life, and neither is going to encroach on the other'. The whole point about informal networking is that it is a way of building trust. If people get to know you and trust you, you will find it easier to influence them. If, however, you never speak about your personal life, always leave work at finishing time, and never get to know your colleagues socially, it's very difficult to build up this kind of relationship. You will therefore find it harder to be influential than someone who has taken the time and trouble to get to know people.

Don't make the mistake of thinking that all men are hostile to having female colleagues. While doing company surveys I have heard men saying things like:

> I am much happier about working in this department now that there are some women around. It's a much more pleasant, human place to be.

Women who are confident enough to speak up, but who don't try to be macho, bring a quality which is missing from all-male groups. Slowly, but surely, the social environment in organisations is changing and women can contribute to and benefit from these changes. Where men complain about female colleagues it is usually aggression that they are reacting against, or the tendency of some women to keep their heads down and stay in the background.

Many senior men are aware of the disadvantages that women face and want to help women whom they see as having potential. The knack is to be alert enough to recognise the help when it comes your way. For example, a suggestion from the boss to write a key report should not be viewed simply as more work, but rather a chance to shine within the organisation. Not only should you be alert to these opportunities, but there is no harm in asking for help in increasing your sphere of influence. Most men will understand and sympathise with your desire to gain a higher profile.

Some of the women I interviewed for this book were aware of the need to be political.

> I am very conscious of opportunities [said Judy Presnell]. Every time you meet someone you are influencing them. So I am conscious of the message I am putting across and I always put the best me forward.

Jennifer Haigh has always perceived the need to use strategy, and now she does it instinctively, but she is still aware that it is harder for women to be influential and, initially at least, must put more of a conscious effort into it. June Campbell agrees:

> Generally, women have to work a little harder to be taken seriously and influence. I try to work out what the other person wants, what I want and then I try to combine the two. You've got to give them something so that they give you what *you* want.

Skills that help us to be influential

The difficulty of being paid attention to as a woman highlights the need to use skilful behaviour so that people will take us seriously and cooperate. No matter what type of person you are, you can find ways of achieving your aims.

Influencing others is a process which can be seen in three stages:

• *Getting in* starts it all off. There you get the other person to pay attention and to give you a chance to influence them.

• *Getting action* is where you influence them to accept your proposal or to act in the way you want them to.

• *Getting out* is the art of leaving the other person genuinely influenced by you, and not inclined to change their mind or give your request low priority.

GETTING IN: HOW TO START INFLUENCING A PERSON
This first stage is vitally important to the process of influencing someone. If you cannot get that person to listen to your proposal and give you a chance to influence them, then you will get nowhere. If you are trying to persuade someone who listens politely but clearly has their mind closed to your proposals right from the start, you have failed. Let's look at what you need to do at this initial getting in stage to make it more likely that you will succeed.

Getting in means dealing with the other person's initial concerns and making a start on building a good working relationship. This depends on four factors:

• *Rapport* This is established by being attentive to the other person, looking at them, listening and responding to them. You need to empathise and encourage them so that they feel you are genuinely interested and concerned. Smiles and eye contact will help. If, instead, you rattle off your arguments with a scowl of concentration, this may be an understandable product of your anxiety, but it will not inspire trust and the other person will be less inclined to give you a chance to influence them. Men are human too, and can be quite intimidated or put off by serious, intense women who do not attempt to build rapport.

● *Anxiety* Anxiety is usually present at the getting in stage. The main cause of this is uncertainty. The other person will remain anxious until they know why you're there and what you're going to ask them to do. You will also be anxious until you have made your intentions clear. So, come to the point early on in your conversation, don't keep them guessing. Also, try to establish what the other person's objectives and concerns are so that you can address them.

● *Trust* The other person needs to trust you before they will do what you ask, particularly if this involves taking risks. You can begin to build trust at an early stage by showing interest, empathy, integrity and openness. If you look a person in the eye and behave as if you have nothing to hide, it is more likely that they will want to trust you. If you avoid eye contact people will think you are devious and untrustworthy.

● *Credibility* Your behaviour is critical in establishing credibility. Being visibly anxious yourself and making an elaborate presentation of your qualifications and expertise is likely to arouse anxiety and distrust. On the other hand, if you walk, speak and sit with the quiet confidence and authority of someone who knows what they are doing then people are more likely to find you credible. Chapter 5 – on managing your image – gives advice on the sort of dress and body language that will increase your standing in the eyes of other people.

Getting in may take a few minutes, several hours or several meetings, but until you have achieved this, you won't be able to exert any influence. Once you begin to see that the other person is opening his or her mind to your proposals, it is time to bring into play your strategy for getting action.

GETTING ACTION: HOW TO CHOOSE YOUR
INFLUENCE STRATEGY
There are two basic approaches.

The push strategy is effective when you know where you want to go or are clear about the solution to the problem. This is a directive strategy in which there are a number of stages:

1. Set the scene, identify the problem or opportunity and make your proposal for the solution.
2. Invite reactions.
3. Summarise your discussions and check that you understand each other.
4. Deal with the objections, either by persuasion or authority, depending on whether you want commitment or compliance.
5. Agree on the outcome – who is going to do what and by when.

It is quite a strong, powerful approach, and the trick is to avoid making the other person feel overwhelmed. Be clear and firm about your proposals, but also be approachable so that the other person can feel free to discuss them and raise any concerns.

Here is an example of the 'push' strategy.

I called in the sales manager and explained that I had noticed several problems with the open-plan layout of the sales department. It was very noisy and untidy and there seemed to be nowhere that people could speak in private for appraisals or counselling or disciplinary interviews. I said that I wanted to change it back to a conventional department with separate offices and asked him what he thought of this. His main worry was that people might become isolated, and communication wouldn't be so easy between staff shut away in different offices.

We discussed this point and then I summarised the discussion like this. 'The main advantage, as I saw it, was that it would encourage more communication of a private and sensitive nature. The main objection to removing open-plan was losing free communication.' I dealt with his objection by saying that we would insist on an open door policy to keep communication flowing freely. Finally, we agreed that he would get some quotes from builders for re-doing the office and we would meet to discuss these in four weeks time.

The 'pull' strategy is quite different as it depends on arriving at a joint agreement on what to do, rather than on one person's

authority. This is most effective when the other person's commitment is essential. This strategy also has several stages:
1. State your view of the problem or opportunity.
2. Clarify how the other person sees the situation.
3. Work for an agreement over the existence of the problem or opportunity.
4. Look for solutions, using as many of the other person's ideas as possible, especially if their commitment is important.
5. Come to a joint agreement on what is going to be done.

The 'pull' strategy calls for quite a different set of skills from the 'push' strategy. Here you need to let them know you are pulling together. You need to be supportive so that the other person is encouraged to make their own suggestions. Where there are differences of opinion you need to look for common ground and build on any aims or interests you share. The most powerful thing you can do is appeal to the other person's imagination. Get them to picture how things could be in the future if you are able to go forward. Once a person starts to build visions of the future, she (or he) is close to being committed. You can help them to do this by painting pictures with words.

This is an example of the 'pull' strategy:

I spoke to one of my supervisors about a problem that he was experiencing in managing his staff. I explained that I had noticed an atmosphere of tension in his section, and four of his staff had complained to me about his blunt manner. I then asked him to tell me how he saw the situation and whether he saw it as a problem.

He was quite upset and defensive at first, but eventually agreed that he was finding it hard. Most of his staff were very young and inclined to be sloppy and irresponsible. He did lose his temper sometimes, because he was always anxious about what they would forget to do next.

I asked him for his ideas about solutions and we explored several possibilities. Finally he said that he thought the main problem was that the staff had never had any proper induction, and were probably sloppy because they had never been taught how to do the job properly. So we agreed to have an induction day where he and I would both go through the work routine with them and answer all their questions. He also agreed to try to be more patient and to adopt more of a role of teacher until everyone was up to scratch.

Interestingly, the solution of having an induction day had not occurred to me before our meeting. I was thinking that maybe he ought to go on a staff management course. But when we looked at the problem together it occurred to us both that the staff really didn't know how to do their jobs properly. The induction day worked well, and the atmosphere in the section is greatly improved.

Many women prefer to use the 'pull' strategy, because of their strong need to be liked and their aversion to power. One advantage of this strategy is that it uses the other person's ideas, which wins their commitment and enriches the final decision. Two heads are better than one. The other advantage is that it develops the other person's ability to work out solutions to problems and make decisions.

There are disadvantages in using the 'pull' strategy all the time:
1. It is inappropriate when quick or routine decisions have to be made.
2. If you always use it you run the risk of being seen as weak and indecisive.

However, it would also be a mistake to use 'push' all the time because your subordinates won't develop, and you may be seen as arrogant and Draconian.

Powerful but effective women use 'pull' frequently, but use their judgement about the circumstances. Many people actually require a more directive 'push' style of influence, and you need to put yourself into their shoes to see how they may be feeling about the situation. Sometimes, even after careful thought, we can still get it wrong:

I went in to see my new boss about introducing a new training scheme into the company. I had done all the research, and knew what was needed. I decided to use the 'pull' strategy because I assumed that my boss would want to have a say about the size and nature of the training scheme. So I presented my findings then proposed that we work together on designing a training programme based on these findings. I couldn't have made a worse mistake! 'You haven't done your homework,' she said. 'I expected you to come here with a proposal for a training programme – you have only done half the work! Please come back when you have finished.' I did what she asked and the second meeting was more successful, but I learnt a lesson from that experience. My assumption that my boss wanted to be involved in the detailed decision-making was wrong. She expected me to use 'push' and thought I was unprepared when I didn't. Now I go prepared to meetings like this. I take my detailed proposals with me and if I see that I am expected to produce them then I can do so.

Not only is the choice of strategy important, but so is your choice of influence style. Here are a number of influence styles you might choose. Put a tick against the styles you normally use in the course of your work.

INFLUENCE STYLES

Coerce
Characteristics:	Insisting, threatening.
Comment:	Can produce resentment or lack of commitment.

Educate
Characteristics:	Providing information, or introducing new concepts.
Comment:	People will learn if your information is seen as relevant. You will be distrusted if there is a conflict of interests.

Sell
Characteristics:	Emphasising benefits.
Comment:	Trust is required – otherwise you will be perceived as manipulative or self-serving.

Rational/Logical
Characteristics:	Argument based on logic and reason.
Comment:	This fails if there is a conflict of interests. It requires a low emotional temperature.

Emotive
Characteristics:	Appeal to feelings and values, especially attempts to make the other party feel guilty.
Comment:	Many people are unable or unwilling to work at a feelings level.

Expert

Characteristics:	Using superior knowledge or expertise.
Comment:	Credibility is required. There is a danger of dependence, and making a scapegoat of the influencer if the solution does not work.

Model

Characteristics:	Providing examples.
Comment:	This creates dependence on the model being present. It is difficult to transfer to a new situation. It can be effective if the model is very impressive and is around long enough.

Charisma

Characteristics:	Use of personality and ego strength.
Comment:	This is liable to produce dependence. The other person can feel let down once the influencer is not there.

Negotiate

Characteristics:	Bargaining.
Comment:	This assumes a rough equality of power. It requires compromise.

Joint problem solving

Characteristics:	Mutual agreement of the best decision.
Comment:	This requires high trust. It can lead to the best available decision and to high commitment. It is time consuming.

Non-directive

Characteristics:	Encourage the other person to develop their own analysis of and solution to the problem.
Comment:	This leads to high commitment to the solution. The influencer has less control over the nature of the solution.

Have a look at the styles which you have ticked and see what they tell you about yourself. If you always prefer to use a 'pull' strategy and influence styles like 'educate', 'joint problem-solving' and 'non-directive', then that may reflect the type of job you have, but it also says something about your personality and about the sorts of relationships you prefer to have with other people. You obviously prefer to share the decision making with others rather than to be directive.

If, on the other hand, you prefer the 'push' strategy and choose influence styles such as 'coerce', 'sell', 'expert', 'model' and 'charisma', then you may be the sort of personality who prefers to lead from the front.

It helps to become aware of your preferences because if you have a tendency to use the same strategy and style with everyone then your success rate may not be high. What influences one person can often fail with another. For example, the use of expertise as a way of influencing works with some people and in some professions, but not in others. Even doctors who used to be able to rely on their expertise as an effective influence style, now find that a well-informed patient will sometimes challenge that expertise. You have to learn to judge which style would be most successful and use it. You will learn from trial and error, but you will make fewer mistakes if you try to put yourself in the other person's shoes. Obviously, some influence styles would not fit with your personality or your work situation, but the longer the list of styles in your repertoire, the more likely you will be to choose the style that matches the situation and brings success:

> Recently I had to persuade three members of my staff to spend more time with our clients and less time in the office. I started off by presenting a rational argument for the need for this change, and two of the staff accepted my argument straightaway. They could see the logic behind the change and were happy to do what I proposed. The third member of staff would not play ball at first. He could see the point but felt he did not know how to go about building up relationships with clients, so argued strongly for being the one to stay behind in the office. I decided to try to use myself as a model, and take him with me to see some of the clients so that he could watch me dealing with them. At first he just watched and said little in these meetings, but as time went on he began to feel he knew what to do and started to speak to the clients. Eventually at his own request I let him go on his own. Now we discuss problems together, but he likes and values this new aspect of his work because he feels confident now that he can do it.

When *you* next have to influence someone, do a bit of preplanning: get your facts together and prepare your case. This will make you more self-confident and credible. Then put yourself in the other person's shoes and choose the strategy (push or pull) and the influence style which is most likely to get through to them. Be alert during your meeting, try to think about how they are reacting and whether your approach is working. Ask them what they think of your proposals and be prepared to change your approach if necessary. This sort of sensitivity to the other person will help you to become more skilful.

GETTING OUT: LEAVING THE OTHER PERSON GENUINELY INFLUENCED

The big question at this final stage is – will the person you have influenced actually do what they have agreed to do? They may come under pressure from other people, or they may forget or not find the time to do what they have promised you they will do. Persistence is often required at this stage. People need to be reminded, given deadlines and reinfluenced in one way or the other. And, most important, they need to be thanked when they have done it.

In a large computer company where I worked for a time, getting out and leaving the other person genuinely influenced was a big problem. Many of the idea-generating jobs were held by clever young people (many of them women). Although they were able to influence senior managers to listen to them, and to acknowledge the potential in many of their ideas, they were not skilled at getting genuine commitment. They would come away from a meeting feeling very pleased that one of their ideas was being developed. But over the months this feeling would turn to bitter disappointment as they realised that nothing was being done.

What was happening was that the managers who could further the ideas, although genuinely impressed by them, were not committed enough to make time for developing those ideas in their busy schedule. The astute person would have booked a second meeting with the manager, at which she worked out in detail the timing and resources needed to develop the project. She would also have established who was in charge, and formed a liaison with that person for monitoring progress. She would have booked regular monthly or quarterly meetings with the manager to discuss the project, and to work out how to overcome setbacks. If this sort of persistence still did not get results, then she would have taken the problem to other senior influential people and asked for their help.

Here is one example from my own early experience of getting out.

In my first senior appointment I had to share a secretary with my boss and colleagues, so when I needed something typed quickly it was always a worry. The competition for the secretary's time was fierce. On one occasion I needed a document typed that same day to meet a very important deadline. I took my script in to the secretary in the morning and explained the urgency. She promised to finish it by the end of the day but I could see she was under pressure from other people. My document was a tender for a large amount of work which, if it met the deadline and was successful, would do wonders for my reputation. So, I found a spare chair in the secretary's office, and spent the day there doing other work. Because I was there, she returned to my work whenever she had had to leave it to type an urgent letter, and when my colleagues came in to her to give her their work she explained that she had to finish mine first. In the afternoon, my boss gave her a long, urgent letter to type and the poor girl tried to get me to extend my deadline to the next day. But I couldn't, and I quietly kept the pressure up. Finally, after tears and panic, she managed to finish my work in time. Had I not stayed with her I would have had no chance.

From that day I learnt just how much persistence you need when the person you think you have influenced has a lot of other pressures. People who are very busy will respond to people with the most power, or the most persistence. In this case all I had was persistence, but I used it and it worked. I gave that secretary my heartfelt thanks – and bought her a box of chocolates!

To summarise: to get things done at work women need to influence other people by getting involved in the informal power groupings which exist in organisations, and by using skilful behaviour strategies. Overcome any distaste you may have for organisation politics and recognise it as a legitimate way of getting things done and being effective. Be sensitive to the other person's concerns and values, and find an approach which takes these into account. When you *need* to be decisive and authoritative, plan your approach. Making this sort of effort will help you to overcome many of the disadantages women face when they are trying to be influential.

4

Assertiveness

ASSERTIVENESS
IS THE DIFFERENCE
BETWEEN
APOLOGY AND ATTILA THE HUN.

Assertiveness is the buzz word of the decade – and it is one of the keys to success. Men are (you guessed it) ambivalent about assertive women. While they don't like women to be fading violets they are a bit nervous about the idea of women standing up for themselves too much. The trouble is that most people don't really know what assertiveness means. I hope to clear up some of this confusion over the meaning of the term and explain why it is that women need to be assertive yet often find it hard to be so. You will find practical guidelines later in this chapter for dealing assertively (and therefore effectively) with some of the difficult situations women have to face at work.

Most people understand that assertion means standing up for yourself, but beyond that there are many misconceptions. 'I'm not going to send her on an assertiveness course – she's too assertive already!' is a comment I hear frequently. In fact, it is not possible to be *too* assertive – because that is a contradiction in terms.

ASSERTION *NOT* AGGRESSION

Assertion is about your external behaviour *and* how you feel inside, about yourself and about the person you are dealing with.

It involves respecting and standing up for your own rights and needs, but also recognising and respecting the rights and needs of the other person. It's usually very clear when someone is being aggressive rather than assertive, although in both cases they are standing up for themselves. An aggressive person will make you feel put down rather than respected. So if a boss says of a woman that she is already too assertive, it may mean that she is violating his rights in some way, and is possibly being slightly aggressive, rather than assertive, in her behaviour.

An aggressive manner dominates, humiliates or degrades the other person and the message you give out is: 'What you want isn't important, and your feelings don't count'.

Many women, when they find themselves in conflict at work, see only two choices:

- To be unassertive and avoid standing up for themselves.
- To stand up for what they think is right, but to be accusatory and aggressive about it.

Either way, they are likely to deal badly with the situation and feel inadequate about it afterwards. Fortunately, there *is* a middle road and you can assert your own rights without denying those of the other person.

Accepting that we have rights in every situation is fundamental to assertive behaviour. Typically, women are brought up thinking that their needs come second, and that in comparison to the people they are dealing with they haven't any rights. The first step towards being assertive is to become aware of your rights and to respect yourself. Here is a list of rights which are held in common by all human beings and which women need to accept as their own.

- The right to be treated with respect.
- The right to have and express your own feelings and opinions.
- The right to be listened to and taken seriously.
- The right to set your own priorities.
- The right to say no without feeling guilty.
- The right to ask for what you want.
- The right to ask for information from professionals.
- The right to make mistakes.
- The right to choose not to assert yourself.[8]

Let's look a little more closely at the sort of attitudes to adopt when you want to be assertive. Your intention is to communicate, to influence, to gain self-respect without diminishing others:

You try to find out what is right rather than who is right.

The tone of your voice is firm but not hostile.

You use gestures and postures which denote strength and confidence, and your speech is fluent, clear and expressive.

Your eye contact is firm, but not a stare-down.

You are aware of, and deal with, feelings as they occur, without denying them.

Tension is kept within a normal, constructive range.

The effect on others will be that they feel informed and enhanced. They will be able to disagree without being seen as attackers or being judged as incompetent, and consequently they will experience you as being more approachable yet influential.

DIRECT AGGRESSION
In contrast, when you are being aggressive the intention is to be 'on top', to put others down. You look after your own interests at the expense of other people's, and your aim is to dominate without being influenced:

Your body language works to demean or dominate the other person.

Eye contact is a stare down and the tone of your voice is strident, sarcastic or condescending.

Tension is turned outwards.

You may be feeling fear, guilt or hurt which has built up over time to boiling point, so your emotional temperature is above normal and is usually expressed by inappropriate anger or hostility.

The effect on others will be that they feel hurt, defensive, fearful or resentful. They can't disagree with you without being seen as presumptuous, incompetent or defensive.

INDIRECT AGGRESSION

While direct aggression feels unpleasant when you're on the receiving end, at least you know where you stand. But there is also indirect aggression, which is much more difficult to deal with. Indirect aggression violates the other person's rights in a subtle, underhand way. It is used by people who are not feeling powerful enough to be directly aggressive. Instead of being openly angry or accusatory they show through their tone of voice, facial expression or actions that they are feeling negative. Sarcasm, door slamming and sulking are all examples of this.

This behaviour is difficult to confront, because even if you ask, 'What's the matter?' the other person can say 'Nothing!' Because women so often feel powerless, we frequently choose indirect aggression instead of assertion or direct aggression. The effect on others may be that it makes them feel guilty, angry or outraged but impotent to deal with the situation. It sours relationships and loses you respect.

NON-ASSERTION

Non-assertion is another form of behaviour used by people who are feeling powerless. The unassertive person does not stand up for their own rights and allows the other person to violate them. They express their thoughts and feelings in such an apologetic, diffident, self-effacing manner that other people can easily disregard them. The message communicated is − 'I don't respect myself; I don't count, so you can take advantage of me.' The goal of non-assertion is to appease others and to avoid conflict.[7]

If you look more closely at non-assertion you will recognise the ways in which you can signal it and the effect it has on others. The intention with non-assertion is to be 'safe', to appease, to let others take responsibility for you, to get sympathy and to deny your own needs. You use such mannerisms as downcast eyes, a slumped body, fidgeting, wringing hands and a whining, hesitant or childish voice. The message is 'I can't contribute much of value, in comparison to you, who are more important.' The effect on others is that they either discount you, or feel guilty and frustrated because they can't disagree without seeming uncaring or hostile. Also, they do not know where they stand because you do not express your needs or point of view. So they end up walking all over you, either because you invite them to, or because you give them no information about your needs.

ASSERTIVE BEHAVIOUR

Assertion is by far the most influential and satisfying way to behave. When you express your needs and point of view you avoid the build-up of frustration and bitterness experienced by unassertive people. And because you treat other people with respect you make allies rather than enemies. Assertive people do not dissipate their energies on internal conflicts, disappointments and tensions, so they have much more energy left over for living and working. Also, other people find them more rewarding and pleasant. People know where they stand if you say what you want, or what is troubling you, without hostility, sulks or whines.

However, many women find it hard to be consistently assertive at work and it is important to understand the main reasons why.

- Our childhood conditioning teaches us that as the nurturing, caring sex our needs come second, and we feel selfish and greedy when we think of ourselves and make demands or say no to a request. By the time we grow up, it is second nature to put our own needs second when dealing with men, or indeed with anyone in authority.
- We tend to put relationships with other people at the top of our priorities. We have career ambitions and achievement goals of course, but our personal relationships often come first. If standing up for ourselves and our beliefs threatens relationships with other people, we are strongly motivated to back down.
- We may also fear unpleasant consequences. Many women are horrified by rows or awkward scenes, so they often choose to say nothing rather than risk unpleasantness.
- Some women are unassertive in order to make themselves invisible, to avoid drawing attention to themselves, because they lack confidence.
- Other women are passive simply because they don't accept that they have any rights.
- Women frequently undervalue their skills and abilities and feel that they have to defer to other people whom they see as being more worthwhile than themselves.

- A final cause for non-assertion is that assertion is sometimes confused with rudeness.

INTERNAL TENSIONS

Initially, passive appeasing behaviour can reduce anxiety and guilt if it helps you to avoid a conflict. In the longer term, however, consistent denial of your needs will lead to a growing loss of self-esteem, frustration and internal tensions. Denying your needs doesn't make them go away, and the resulting build-up of anger, hurt and stress drains your energy. Over time, this build-up of internal tensions makes it even harder for you to behave assertively, and may lead to health problems.

Consistent, unassertive behaviour will sometimes lead to sudden aggressive outbursts from the person who has reached the point where she can take no more. This outburst will come as a surprise to others, who won't have been aware of ignoring her needs, because she has been doing nothing to express them.

Unfortunately, aggression is as counterproductive as non-assertion in that it creates bad feelings all round. Women who find it hard to be consistently assertive will not only be unassertive, they will often be aggressive too.

There is a tendency for some women in work to be aggressive much of the time. This is very understandable when you consider the difficult, threatening circumstances isolated 'token' women have to face. People are often aggressive when they feel threatened and insecure. Sometimes women are aggressive because they feel, from watching their male peers, that it is 'the only way to get things done'. Also, women frequently respond aggressively when they feel unfairly treated, 'put down' or discriminated against.

However justifiable the causes of aggression, in the end it is counterproductive. It may, in the short-term, release some pent-up emotions, and give you a sense of power if you get the result you want. In the medium or long-term you will feel ashamed of your behaviour and suffer from guilt. You may turn these feelings outward and blame others and find yourself hating or mistrusting them. Aggressive behaviour will eventually increase the isolation you experience, because it causes problems with friends and colleagues.

Aggressive men also feel ashamed, and suffer from isolation, but because they usually have less invested in personal relationships than women, their problems may not be as intensely felt.

Practical assertion techniques

It is not enough simply to say that non-assertion and aggression should be avoided. Most of us realise this anyway. The problem is that all too frequently situations arise that are difficult to cope with, and you may find yourself acting aggressively or unassertively even though your initial intention was to be assertive.

Learning a few assertiveness techniques will help you to be more effective.

● *Basic Assertion* There are different ways of being assertive and if you choose this basic direct method you may run the risk of being seen as aggressive. Here is an example:

It's hot and stuffy in this room so I am going to open the window.

If it is said in a direct, down-to-earth and pleasant way, then you are expressing your needs and asserting your rights without violating the rights of the other people in the room. If your tone of voice denotes assertion rather than aggression, then you make it possible for other people to disagree without feeling either intimidated or hostile. However, basic assertion does leave a lot of room for misinterpretation. If the tone of voice is slightly strident, or if the other person does not expect you as a woman to be asserting your rights, then you may be seen as aggressive.

● *Responsive Assertion* With this form of assertion you state your needs, and then check with the other person that you aren't violating theirs.

It's hot in this room. I'm going to open the window. Is that OK with you?

This statement makes it clear that you are inviting the other person to say what they want. Of course, if they disagree about the room temperature you will have to negotiate a compromise. But you have expressed your needs and shown clearly that you respect the needs of the other person, so that it is less likely you will be misconstrued as being aggressive.

● *The 'Broken Record' Response* This is useful in dealing with people who are being manipulative or devious. On many occasions I have found myself making a justified complaint to someone who evades answering my points and who tries to counter attack with criticisms or irrelevant arguments. It is all too easy to get caught with these irrelevancies and end up in bitter arguments about side issues. When this happens to me we both get angry and I do not end up getting a satisfactory response to my complaint.

Think of the times you have tried to return something you have bought and the salesman twists and turns and evades acknowledging the fault in the product, making it difficult for you to get satisfaction. It is all too easy to have an embarrassing row which may not get the results you want.

'Broken Record' is marvellously effective in these situations. Simply choose a relevant phrase with which you feel comfortable and, without getting angry or loud, repeat this assertive statement each time the person tries to persuade you to change your mind.

If you remain firm on this original statement, and resist the temptation to answer or respond to possible insults, you will eventually convince the other person that you are not prepared to be ignored or diverted. If you do allow the other person to 'hook' you into arguing over one of their diversionary points, then you end up getting nowhere, or allowing them to manipulate you out of your rights.

Broken records eventually get heard – because it is uncomfortable to listen to them for too long! It is such a simple technique, yet so powerful and effective. It is also a wonderful way of keeping control of the situation and of your emotions. I can still remember how pleased I was with its results the first time I used it. By mistake, I had parked my car in a private car park and it had been locked in. 'Please will you let me get it out,' I said to the attendant after apologising. 'I need it to get back to work.' I listened politely to his abuse of my character and his insistence that he wouldn't let me get the car out that day. But instead of arguing with him or defending myself I just kept repeating my request. Eventually, in response to my control and lack of hostility he calmed down and we parted on good terms. I got my car. Had I become aggressive I'm sure my car would have spent a long time in that car park.

Here is another example of a broken record in action. This conversation was between Marsha, a supervisor in a Civil Service department, and a clerical officer whose timekeeping was very bad:

'Johnny, you have been coming in up to thirty minutes late most days for the last two weeks. I'm going to have to insist that you turn up by nine o'clock.'

'Come on, Marsha, you know how difficult it is for me. It's so hard to get up early, and even if I do the trains often let me down.'

'I know it's not easy, but you've got to overcome these problems and turn up on time.'

'Look, I try, you know, but all sorts of things crop up to delay me. Just yesterday my son announced as I was leaving the house that he hated school and wanted to stop going. What could I do but stay and talk? The child is only ten.'

'That couldn't have been easy for you, Johnny, but you'll have to find solutions that don't make you late for work.'

'You are a hard woman, Marsha. It's OK for you, you don't have a wife and kids hanging round your ankles in the mornings. I think you could allow me to be late now and again.'

'I'm sorry, Johnny, I know I'm not asking you to do something easy, but you've got to start turning up on time.'

'Well, OK. I guess I'll have to start getting up even earlier to make sure I always catch the eight-fifteen train.'

'That's great, Johnny. I'm sure I can count on you to stick to the nine o'clock start time.'

LEARNING TO SAY 'NO'
Another typical problem for women at work is that they find it difficult to say 'no', because they hate to risk causing offence or hurting people's feelings. The trouble is that there are many occasions at work when you need to say no, and if you can't you will simply be ineffective.

Learn to say no assertively, in a way which causes no offence. Of course the other person will still be disappointed, but if you handle it assertively they won't feel badly about it. Here are the guidelines for saying no assertively.

- Decide for sure that you want to say no. If you are uncertain, ask for time to think it over.
- Use no in your answer so that the other person is quite clear that you mean no.
- Use empathy because this makes your refusal much more acceptable.

- If you have some ideas about other ways of solving the problem then discuss them with the other person.

For example, Stella is a transport manager, and someone from another department is asking for a driver and vehicle to do a job for him.

'Stella, I need a van and a driver for the day after tomorrow to take this rush job to South Wales.'

'I'm sorry Mike, all the vehicles are fully booked until Friday – I'll have to say no this time.'

'Hey come on Stella, I'm sure you could help me with a bit of creative thinking. I'm really in a jam.'

'I realise you've got a problem. Mike and I very much regret not being able to help you out, but all the vans are already booked to high-priority jobs.'

'Christ, that really leaves me in a mess.'

'Look Mike, I can't help you with my vehicles but maybe we can work out another way to solve the problem.'

'I'd really be glad if we could Stella, I'm desperate.'

'Why not use a reliable sub-contractor? I could give you a few phone numbers.'

'Why didn't *I* think of that! I'll give it a try. Thanks.'

In this case Stella made it very clear that she was saying no, but by using empathy she made her refusal more acceptable to Mike, even though he was disappointed. Had she not used empathy, her refusal would have seemed much harsher and Mike may have become aggressive. By suggesting another solution, Stella avoided an unpleasant confrontation. Of course, she would have avoided this by saying yes, but then she would have put herself in an impossible situation as she really didn't have a van to spare.

'FOGGING'

Successful working women can pose a threat to men and to women who live their lives differently, and they often come in for unjustified criticism. When this happens it is all too easy to develop feelings of guilt or insecurity, become defensive, make excuses or get involved in arguments that lead nowhere.

The technique called 'fogging' can be used to deal with this sort of manipulative criticism. It is not to be used where the criticism is valid, however. 'Fogging' enables you to have a defence against those who may try to influence you to behave in a certain way by criticism. By using this technique you create a 'fog bank' which can make it impossible for a critic to have any success. While acknowledging to the critic that there may be some truth in what he or she is saying, you remain your own judge of what you do. The technique allows you to receive criticism comfortably without becoming anxious and defensive, but gives no reward or encouragement to the person using manipulative criticism.

Here are some examples of how the technique may work:

'Isn't it about time you gave up work and started a family? I really think it's unfair to poor Bob for you to be such a dedicated career woman.'
'I can understand why you should feel that way.'

'You often get over-emotional, just like a typical woman.'
'You may be right.'

In each case the attacker is stopped in his tracks by your fog bank. You have failed to provide him or her with ammunition for further attack by not denying the criticism. You haven't become defensive, which would have implied that the criticism was justified. And you avoided the temptation to respond with counter criticism and so start a row.

Having defused the criticism with the fogging technique you have avoided wasting your energy and emotions on a futile argument, and you can now carry on to discuss something more productive as no one has lost face or become angry.

HANDLING CRITICISM
Receiving *justified* criticism can be difficult for many working women. They feel very guilty when they make a mistake, or do something less than perfectly, and find it hard to accept the criticism assertively. Many women feel that they have to be that much better than their male peers, and dread being less than excellent. They therefore find it hard to accept valid criticism without letting it escalate, and are manipulated through their feelings of guilt or anxiety into either endlessly trying to explain or

seek forgiveness for their error or denying the error through defensiveness and counter-criticism. In either case they cope poorly, impress no one, and feel worse. Men don't like criticism either, but it doesn't normally make them feel so bad. They seem to know that other men think they are all right, in spite of their error.

In order to cope assertively with valid criticism you have to remind yourself that one of your fundamental human rights is the right to make a mistake. You also have to recognise that there is a tendency to feel guilty because you were taught in childhood to feel guilty. However, as an adult, you need to cope with your errors as errors, no more or no less. In other words, assertively accept those things that are negative about yourself.

It will help you to do this if you put your mistakes in the context of all the good work you have done and if you remember all the times you got it right. For example when you are being criticised, possibly in a hostile way for an error you have just made, you can say something like:

'What a stupid mistake, I'm sorry. This is what I'm going to do to put it right. . . .'

This stops you getting into lengthy justifications over how you came to make the mistake and focuses on solving the problem. If you handle criticism in a mature, self-respecting, assertive way it may even turn a negative situation into an opportunity for creating a favourable impression.

Here is an approach taken by one of the interviewees:

I try to deal with people who question my decisions in a down-to-earth, assertive way. I don't get defensive about the implied criticism. Instead I try to share my objectives with them and turn it into a joint venture for finding a better solution by asking, 'What would you do in my position?'

A woman in publishing had this experience:

When I was at my last job I failed to spot a spelling mistake on one of my brochures before it went to print. Unfortunately, the managing director – who vetted all brochures – spotted the mistake first. He hit the roof. In fact it was my boss who got the full blast of his fury and he came straight to me and told me off.

I felt terrible, it was such an unnecessary mistake, and such an expensive one. Thousands of these brochures had been printed. I could have got very defensive, especially as I was pregnant and not feeling at my best. But I choked back my feelings and said, 'That's absolutely terrible. It is completely my fault and I am very sorry.'

I couldn't really do anything to put it right because the brochures had to be thrown away and reprinted. But I decided the least I could do was to speak to the managing director. I took my courage in my hands and went to his office and said, 'I am the culprit who produced those brochures with the mistake. I have no excuse, it was sloppy of me and I have come to say how sorry I am.'

He was silent for a moment and I half-expected to get the sack, but instead he just said, 'Yes, it was sloppy but we all make mistakes. I'm sure this is one you won't make again.'

Coping with anger

Often when someone is criticising you, their insecurity, anxiety or lack of trust will express itself as anger or hostility. When you notice these strong negative emotions being directed at you, it is important to give the person a chance to express their feelings and talk about the problem *before* trying to deal with it in a practical way. Anger is a strong emotion and it has a distinct effect on the body which makes it difficult for the angry person to think and behave rationally. They need to be given a chance to 'get it off their chest' and cool down before you can begin to deal with the problem effectively.

In order to cope with an angry, hostile person you must first cope with your own feelings. Distance yourself psychologically from the anger. Try to work out what is happening instead of becoming emotionally involved. In this way you can avoid being paralysed by the anger and instead can concentrate on reacting appropriately.

If you are in charge of your own feelings it will be easier for you to follow these four guidelines.

- Let the angry person express their feelings. If you try to disallow their anger or tell them not to shout it will only make them angrier. Just listen attentively to what they are saying.
- Try to find out why they are angry. Ask questions and summarise what they are saying so that they can see that you are

trying to understand. Do this in a way that is neither conde-scending nor judgemental.
- Don't argue back; this will only prolong the agony. Express your own feelings, but don't surrender to them.
- When you see that they have calmed down, because you gave them the time and opportunity to express their anger, then you can reduce the threat you pose to them. This may mean apologising, explaining, agreeing to behave differently or sug-gesting some other solution to the problem.

One female director sometimes has to deal with angry complaints over the telephone. First of all she says, 'Please help me to understand the problem.' When she is clear about the specifics of the complaint she then says, 'I'll make sure that something is done about it.' She always reports back. She keeps in constant touch with dissatisfied clients. She uses these tactics to diffuse their anger instead of getting defensive or overapologetic.

THE VALUE OF HUMOUR
Successful women are always having to cope with the assumption by other people that women are low status. It is as if the rest of the world cannot resist taking cracks at us from time to time for stepping out of role. It happens so frequently that it is worth finding an assertive way of dealing with it that doesn't waste energy or create unnecessary enemies. Stand up for yourself in a humorous, pleasant way and keep it light.

When Judy Presnell walked into the management dining room for the first time after her promotion, the canteen lady said, 'Oh! You're not supposed to come in here.' Judy just laughed and said, 'Oh yes I am,' and walked cheerfully in. The canteen lady realised her mistake, and was not made to lose face or apologise.

Carey Labovitch often finds that people assume she is a secre-tary. She is usually amused and prefers to deal with put-downs in a straightforward, conversational way. Jean Denton has also had to deal with put-downs during her career:

When I first arrived at Austin Rover a male subordinate greeted me with this statement, 'I've worked for two women before – one was my mother and one was my wife.' I just treated it as a joke. I think that women need to use humour much more than they do.

One interviewee went to a major tennis tournament with a male director of her company, as a guest of a business contact of his.

> My host (who didn't know me) turned to the women in the party and said, 'You ladies look very brown. Obviously you are all housewives at home with the time to sit in the sun.' I didn't want to embarrass his non-working wife so I waited a few moments before I smilingly said, 'Actually I'm not a housewife, I'm a director of the company, like Wallace, but I have been on holiday recently.'

Each of these women found a way to assert their status without making the other person feel offended or embarrassed. They used humour to avoid tension in what were potentially awkward situations.

It's not always necessary to be humorous. Often keeping your tone light and avoiding getting the other person's back up will do. Aileen Egan had these two experiences to recount.

> 'I had to speak to one of my staff who wasn't pulling her weight. I said, 'We've got a problem here. I often have to come back to you with work which you haven't done. Would you like to tell me why this is so?' By taking this approach I got the girl to talk to me about the situation and eventually, after some backsliding, she improved.
>
> On another occasion a senior secretary came to me and said she didn't want to work for me. Nothing personal, but she didn't want to work for a woman. I said, 'I'm sorry to hear that. Give it a week and think about it. I hope you'll change your mind.' She did.

Sophie Mirman prefers to stay cool when people are aggressive towards her.

> When I meet aggression I don't get aggressive myself. I stay calm and confront the person assertively. I say, 'I don't like your attitude.' It usually works in toning down their aggression.

THE CARER UNCARING

There is a natural tendency for women to feel guilty about behaving in an uncaring way. They often go through agonies when they have to discipline or dismiss someone, and it's even worse if that person is a man. One woman gave a very revealing account of her recent experience of dismissing a male subordinate. Her boss offered to do it for her but she decided to do it herself.

It was a tricky situation for me. I was this man's immediate boss. When my job was originally advertised he had hoped to get it, but I was given it instead. It soon became clear to me that this man was not up to his job and would have to go. I didn't like having to do it at all. It meant telling him about his inadequacies and I felt he would not take this well from a woman. He was, after all, in quite a senior job himself. I knew he was having problems at home as well, and this didn't make it any easier.

I was very fearful of the dismissal interview. I expected him to break down or be very angry. I find it very hard to handle male aggression. In fact he was not as angry, emotional or as aggressive as I had expected him to be. We often build things up in our minds to be much worse than they actually are.

I felt very self-conscious throughout the interview. I tried to be assertive, but my fear made my voice weak and quivering. I didn't panic but my heart was pounding in my rib cage. At the end I felt I had done my best. I was hesitant, but I didn't lose my temper or get personal when he challenged me. I felt very pleased afterwards that I had faced the hurdle and succeeded in doing something that I found frightening.

There are bound to be times in your career when you cannot overcome your conditioning, and therefore feel frightened or unassertive even though you know it is not rational to do so. Take the plunge, as this woman did, and behave as assertively as you know how, even if you are feeling terrified inside. Your feelings will probably reduce the effectiveness of your performance, but you will feel more confident the next time.

Inner confidence

Assertiveness is about taking risks in your dealings with other people. Why should this be? Standing up for yourself often feels risky because a little voice in your head says things like: 'You can't do that, he'll get very angry and you won't be able to cope' or

'Watch your step here, this person is very important and you can't risk offending her.' In fact, these inner voices are a relic from childhood, when speaking up often meant getting into trouble with people who did have a lot of power over you, like parents and teachers. Now, as an adult, the risks are not anything like so great, but the inner voices continue to give their warnings. Become aware that they are often giving inappropriate warnings. Instead of being ruled by the anxiety caused by this inner dialogue, confront the warnings and rationally assess the degree of risk. If your risk analysis leads you to think that it's worth taking action and doing or saying the frightening thing, then do so. That is the way you will build up your inner confidence and learn to be more assertive.

Being assertive with people who are authority figures – bosses, teachers, administrators, doctors and lawyers for example – may seem risky to some women:

- Since the authority figure possesses certain types of power, women often concede special human rights to him or her, and in comparison diminish their own rights. In reality the person in authority may possess greater power, but not greater rights.
- Some women believe that if they behave in ways that are unpopular with the authority figure then this person will use his or her power against them. This is a possibility and should be taken into account. However, it is the expectation of negative consequences rather than their likelihood that prevents women from asserting themselves with powerful people. In fact, people in authority tend to respond favourably to assertive requests or disagreements when they are made at the appropriate place and time. Many bosses bemoan the fact that their staff are insufficiently assertive with them, and that as a result they only find out what their subordinates think or feel when they hear it through the grapevine. These bosses have more respect for people who have the courage to disagree with them, and much less for those who don't.

I would caution you against asserting yourself routinely or unnecessarily simply to prove that you can do so! There is nothing to be gained, except a reputation as a nuisance, by asserting yourself with your boss about every detail of your job. Be assertive when you have an important concern to voice, and then your boss will pay attention.

Your weak points

If you want to make a start at behaving more assertively at work look at the questionnaire below[9] and answer the questions that are relevant for you. When you have done this, underline those questions for which you have answered 'seldom' or 'never'. These are the situations in which, at present, you find it difficult to be assertive.

		Never	Sometimes	Often
1	When your boss or colleague makes an unreasonable request, can you refuse?			
2	Can you criticise your colleagues – face to face?			
3	Can you discuss openly with a person his/her criticism of your work?			
4	Can you accept a compliment without embarrassment?			
5	Can you state your dissatisfactions at work to your boss?			
6	Are you able to avoid being exploited or pushed around by other people?			
7	Are you able to reprimand a man who is your junior?			
8	Are you able to reprimand a woman who is your junior?			
9	Can you speak up and ask questions at a meeting?			
10	Can you say 'no' when you would like to do so?			
11	When a person is blatantly unfair, do you usually say something about it to him/her?			
12	Can you respond with humour when someone puts you down?			

	Never	Sometimes	Often
13 Can you talk about your feelings of competition with another colleague with whom you feel competitive?			
14 Can you ask whether you have offended someone?			
15 Are you confident in interviews?			
16 Can you get people to listen to your ideas?			
17 When someone justifiably criticises you, can you listen to the criticism without becoming defensive?			
18 When someone completes a task or job for you with which you are dissatisfied can you ask for it to be done correctly?			
19 Do you feel poised and confident among strangers?			
20 If a colleague betrays your confidence, do you tell him/her how you really feel?			
21 If someone you respect expresses opinions with which you strongly disagree, do you state your own point of view?			
22 Are you able to contradict a domineering person?			
23 You hear that another person is spreading false rumours about you. Would you go to him/her directly to correct the situation?			
24 Can you avoid being overly apologetic?			
25 Can you ask people to do you a favour?			

You may not be able to work on all your problem areas straight away, especially if your list is rather long. Choose the least risky and threatening situations first, and when you have built up your confidence with a few successful experiences, move on to the harder ones. Training courses will also be a great help, especially courses specifically for women.

This is how the questionnaire was used by a woman who encountered it on an assertiveness course. It helped her to see that her biggest problems were in these areas:

She could not accept a compliment without embarrassment.
She was unable to avoid being exploited or pushed around by other people.
She found it difficult to speak up and ask questions at a meeting.
She could not say 'no' when she wanted to.
She was unable to contradict a domineering person.
She found it hard to ask people to do her a favour.

The three least risky situations for her were accepting a compliment, saying 'no', and asking people favours. She decided to work on these first because the other areas were too emotionally laden. With accepting compliments, she tried to smile and to say thank you, and to avoid the urge to deny the compliment. With saying 'no' she found she could do this as long as she was empathetic and able to help the person to solve the problem in another way. She slowly learnt to ask people to do her a favour by convincing herself that she had the right to ask, just as they had the right to say 'no'. Once she began to feel that they could say 'no', without it implying a personal rejection, she became more courageous.

Interestingly, once she began to say 'no' and to ask for favours and to feel good about compliments she stopped feeling that she was being exploited or pushed around all the time. So one of the really difficult problems was solved without her needing to work on it directly.

That left speaking in meetings and contradicting a domineering person. She couldn't tackle these before she had built up some confidence by learning to accept compliments and say 'no'. Once the confidence started to grow she managed to speak a little in meetings by preparing what she wanted to say beforehand and finding the courage to say it. It took her six months before she felt able to contradict her domineering colleague. But she finally managed to say to him one day: 'I don't agree entirely with that point. I like the colour you're proposing but I think it needs to be a lighter shade.'

To her surprise he looked at her and said, 'You have a good point there!'

Becoming more assertive is partly a question of learning new skills in the way you deal with other people. But to be assertive you sometimes have to deal with powerful emotions that otherwise prevent you from behaving skilfully.

This interviewee has gone a long way in learning how to overcome her emotional blocks.

> I used to find all situations where I was dealing with people other than my family really fraught. My blunt manner used to make people react badly to me because they saw me as superconfident and threatening. They thought I was aggressive and so they were aggressive back to me. I simply thought that they didn't like me and the fear, stress and anxiety I felt were exhausting and made me appear even more aggressive.
>
> Once I realised that people were nasty to me because they found me threatening, I began to moderate my behaviour. I became more supportive and learnt to show other people that I was interested in them and admired their work.
>
> This has literally changed my life. I am now no longer tied up inside with the fear that people won't like me. I think more about the other person and how they're feeling and adjust my behaviour accordingly. I don't always have to put on a performance. Social situations can still be fraught for me. But I now have something to fall back on. I'm better at understanding what is going on.

Don't give up if you find it hard at first. Remember, the habits of a lifetime's way of thinking and conditioning will not go away overnight. But the nice thing about assertiveness is that when you do use it, it makes the situation so much easier to handle. It makes you feel so much better that you feel encouraged to keep on being assertive in the future.

5

*Managing
your image*

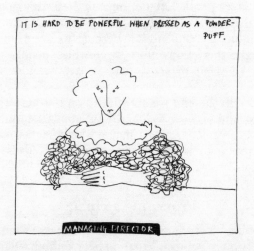

IT IS HARD TO BE POWERFUL WHEN DRESSED AS A POWDER-PUFF.

MANAGING DIRECTOR

The theme of this chapter is how we signal to the outside world through the way that we stand, sit, move and dress, that we are powerful, influential, assertive – and feminine. But why should it be necessary for women to manage their image, and the way they present themselves to the outside world?

'Why can't people just take me as I am?' I hear women say. 'I don't want to pretend to be someone I'm not.'

The answer is that people are so accustomed to treating women as being of low status and powerless that they tend, automatically, to behave in this way, unless we do something to make them think differently. A colleague of mine went to an interview recently and, at the end, was taken aback when the interviewer said, 'You really know what you're talking about! You sound as if you've actually been into those machine shops.' My colleague is an experienced consultant yet, because she was a woman, her interviewer had made an initial assumption that she would have no experience of an engineering factory. He couldn't imagine that she had actually been on a factory floor and he didn't begin to see her as credible until she had spent an hour talking about her work experience. And it is not just men who make such assumptions. Remember the canteen lady who tried to keep Judy Presnell out of the management dining room? She couldn't imagine that a woman belonged in there.

When we manage our image, we are not pretending to be someone that we're not. On the contrary, we are making it clear to the world that we are exactly what we are: competent, experienced, credible people. And it is because we are women that we have to make this extra effort to convince people to take us seriously. We need to show that we are *not* low status and powerless.

Of course, in the end we are judged on our performance, on what we say and on how we handle situations we find ourselves in. However, projecting an image which makes us look as powerful and high status as we wish to be gives us a tremendous head start.

Projecting an image

The first thing you have to do is to establish just what sort of an image you want to project. What do people think when you walk into a room?

Is it, 'This is probably the secretary, or an assistant', or, 'I wonder if she would like to go out with me tonight'? Or could it be 'This is somebody senior and important. I had better pay attention.'?

What do you *want* people to think when you walk into a room? Having read thus far, probably you will want them to think, 'Here is an intelligent, lively looking woman whom I would like to get to know better and to work with,' and, 'She looks like somebody with status and credibility. I ought to take her seriously.' Before you get any further into this chapter why not write down a few sentences which describe the sorts of things you would like people to think about you as a first impression.

Deciding on the image you really want to present will give you something to aim for. But maybe we should further refine this picture of ourselves by asking the question, 'What is an appropriate image for a successful woman?'

I asked the women I interviewed what they thought about this and their answers were fairly consistent. One young woman in a marketing company took her image management very seriously:

It is very important that you look the part if you have a senior position. I wear high-heeled shoes because I am short and don't feel comfortable in flat heels. Plain colours are good for a working woman, but also bright white or strong colours. I like to make a mark with what I wear. The right clothes give you such confidence!

Make-up is important too. Women look much better when they wear it. It would be good to have a few lessons on how to apply it properly – not lots of make-up but clever make-up.

Briefcases are important too. A smart one can make such a difference to your status.

I find it is to my advantage to look attractive. It helps me to win people over, not only because they find me attractive but because they enjoy working with me. But the attractive element is not the answer on its own. I have heard it said that some men find pretty women slightly intimidating.

I've never been propositioned by a man at work, in spite of making every effort to look attractive and well turned out. I think that men back off a little when they are dealing with a successful woman. They treat me with respect rather than flirt with me.

Another woman in her twenties had a more informal approach to managing her image, even though she is very senior. She works in publishing, where an individual style matters.

I sometimes work in jeans, or certainly whatever I feel comfortable in. When I need to impress people I wear young designer clothes. Most of my wardrobe is black and white – these colours look smart both in the day and in the evening. All of my shoes are black.

I also often wear a big black belt and a brooch, because they smarten up anything, even a T-shirt. I wear lots of cotton and prefer baggy clothes and big jackets because they make me look bigger than I am and this gives me a sense of power. But I hate high-heeled shoes and always wear flat heels.

A manager in a financial company comments on body language as well as dress.

I try to hold my back up straight and avoid slouching. I also look people in the eye. I think this gives me status. If I want the person I am with to relax then I use more open body language. I try to look powerful but approachable.

I like to wear high profile clothes so that people realise I am a manager. I wear suits in the winter. When I took up my first management post I bought a suit with a red jacket and a black skirt, and a new smart briefcase. I wanted to give a first impression that said I was a businesswoman, and would make people remember me.

Managing your image is about getting all the detail right. I change my outdoor shoes and do my hair in the ladies room, not in the office. I leave any shopping bags in my locker. They don't do my image any good. In fact I've learnt to avoid saying things like, 'I'm going shopping, or going to get my hair done.' But it seems to be OK to say I'm going to my aerobics class! This is all part of the high profile language which helps to give you a senior image around here.

In the summer I dress less formally but I don't wear revealing clothes and I never wear trousers. I try to always look nice.

One woman at board director level felt she had reached a stage in her career where she could afford to be herself.

I am a very straight person and don't pretend to be what I am not. I look people in the eye because that gives the right impression about me. The only time I cover-up is when I am seething inside. Then I try to look calm and cool because I want to project the image that I am in control and can handle the situation.

I dress fairly informally, but in high-quality natural materials. My clothes are always in and out of the dry cleaners. I wear the bright colours that I like – I don't like drab city clothes. I focus on what suits me rather than what is expected.

Another board director felt that it is very important for women to learn to project a favourable image.

I try to avoid looking scruffy. I wear tights even in the summer. I hate it, but it makes you look professional. You've got to be well-packaged. Sometimes you've got to do things like getting up early in the morning to wash your hair because you know it looks better clean. Don't try to be a clone. If you wear clothes that are feminine but practical you won't make many mistakes.

Finally, here is a woman who moved away from the slightly male image she used to have, even though she works in an engineering environment.

I still wear a suit when I want to be one of the men, as it carries an air of authority. But I have moved away from the slightly male picture I used to present. I prefer to wear more feminine suits now.

Wear nice colours, but avoid ones that are so dominant that business would take second place. There must be a theme to what you wear; either matching colours or a successful contrast. This says that you are well organised. It is also important to look well groomed. In any environment, a scruffy woman would be unacceptable to men.

Body language also says a lot about you. I avoid crossing my arms across my chest because that makes me look defensive. I also avoid excessive hand gestures as they are uncool. I want to look confident, so I make sure I sit comfortably in the chair and don't move too much. I don't use energy unnecessarily when I am stressed, I prefer to look and stay calm and stand back and analyse.

Although these women have some differences in their priorities, they all want to look professional, memorable, and feminine. They all thought that their image was important, and that clothes played a key role in projecting it. They were grappling with the difficulty of arriving at an image which was both powerful and feminine, and used their clothes to reflect this. Mostly they felt the need to wear clothes that were tailored and smart, but they sought ways of softening their outfits to look more feminine.

To achieve an image that is both business-like and feminine is quite difficult. It does mean being clear about definitions of femininity that are appropriate in the business world. We need to steer away from a weak frilly image, or a harsh male macho image. We also have to face up to the dilemma that if we are very sexually attractive to men, then we may not seem powerful and influential to them. We must strike a balance – to be attractive, but not distractingly so. We must also guard against fading into the background and becoming invisible in an attempt not to appear like a siren.

FITTING IN WITH YOUR WORKING ENVIRONMENT

First and foremost, you need to have an image which is appropriate to your environment, your type of work, and your personality.

An appropriate image in the financial world of the city, for example, can be quite wrong in the world of marketing and advertising. A woman friend who had a good job in the City recently applied for a post in a marketing and public relations consultancy. For the interview she dressed soberly but smartly in the clothes she normally wore when meeting clients from finance houses. She also wore black, low-heeled shoes, little jewellery and carried a black briefcase. She behaved in her usual powerful, forthright, positive way, and did quite a lot of talking at the interview. In other words she presented an image which worked for her in the City, and gave the impression in that world that she was credible, confident and senior.

The interviewer in the marketing company saw her in a completely different light. He felt that she talked too much, was overbearing, and dressed dowdily. Senior women in marketing and public relations present themselves quite differently. They dress fashionably and wear the sort of jewellery that you notice (usually large and chunky). They put a lot of effort into being approachable and pleasant, but bright. They tend to do a lot of listening and smiling and are more inclined to let their client do most of the talking.

A contact at a large accountancy company told me of the trouble he was having with one of his female subordinates who came from America. This very competent woman dressed and behaved in a high profile way that was appropriate in New York, but off-putting to people in the more conservative world of accountancy in Britain. Her jewellery and dress had to become less showy, and her manner less direct and blunt, in order to give the image which people here associate with senior accountants from reputable firms. Yet she had enjoyed a successful career in America, so her self-presentation had obviously been right for that country.

It may help you to study what other senior women are wearing in your type of work. A version of this, modified to suit your personality, may be the right way for you to dress. Observe the behaviour of all the senior women you come into contact with, or whom you see on the television. Ask yourself, what do they do to signal the fact that they are senior? If there are some that you admire, they may be good models for you.

Body language

Having defined an image which is powerful but feminine and true to yourself, the next question is how to achieve it. Body language is about:

- Eye contact.
- Facial expressions.
- Posture.
- Gestures and mannerisms.
- Tone of voice.

In fact, it is about everything that gives a message about you to the other person, other than the actual words you use. For example, it says whether you are at ease, or threatened and vulnerable; if you feel sure of yourself or uncertain; whether you are assertive, aggressive or unassertive. Your body language gives signals about your emotional state, your self-confidence, your status and power, whether you are in control or not, whether you are open or not, and whether you are flexible or rigid. Without ever having been formally taught, most people can instinctively tell from your body language how you are feeling about them, and how you are feeling about yourself. The interesting thing about body language is that when it is giving a message which conflicts with what you are saying, it is the body language that people pay attention to. In these situations they don't believe your words.

A simple example of this is when somebody asks you how you are feeling. If you say, 'fine', but use a low, depressed voice, they will probably say, 'No you're not. What's the matter?'

It's not surprising that women often show through their body language that they are unsure of themselves and lacking in confidence. We are conditioned by society to be the second sex. We are not groomed, as many men are from childhood, for senior jobs.

Try spending a day observing your own gestures and movements, and those of other women. Compare these with what you see men doing and you will probably spot some interesting differences.

Successful men are inclined to use gestures that denote strength, are less hesitant, more decisive. They use their hands less often when they are speaking, and only emphasize the occasional point in this way. They tend to look you in the eye, stand up straight and look more in control.

Working women are confident and poised some of the time, but they give themselves away more often than men do. Consider the practised over-animation displayed by some women but not by men. Toying with a strand of hair, or vigorous head nodding, are mannerisms that men studiously avoid. When we are feeling unsure of ourselves, our movements are often jerky and hesitant, and we may twist a ring or fidget with a necklace. These feminine gestures invite attention to our sexuality, and they may even seem like invitations.

The point is that it does not help us, as business women, to overstate these sex differences through our behaviour at work. We don't want to behave exactly like men either, so the balance that we seek for in our self-image needs to be represented by a similar balance in our body language. If we feel we are professional, powerful and feminine, body language has got to show this to the world.

I can remember a time when my body language did me no good at all. I had made an appointment to see someone and when I turned up at his office he attacked me for not coming the previous week, which was when *he* thought we had made the appointment. I don't usually make mistakes like that and suspected him of being in the wrong but I decided to go for an agreement that either of us could have made the mistake and that we should write it off and get down to business. I said all the right things but my body language let me down. My speech was hesitant, and my movements were awkward, I kept fiddling with my ring and I couldn't stop shifting around in my chair. He took all of this anxiety as an admission of guilt on my part. The next time someone wrong foots me I'll stay absolutely still, speak very firmly and look them in the eye.

NERVOUS MANNERISMS

The first stage in managing your image is to avoid girlish, nervous mannerisms. This is not going to be easy because you may often be unaware that you are using them.

> When I am making a presentation, I really have to watch my nervous mannerisms. My hands mostly get me into trouble. I once had a speech recorded on the video and when I watched it afterwards I saw that I was using my hands to conduct the conversation! What a great impression that gave.

> I used to teach evening classes in economics. I was always a bit nervous about lecturing and one night I was fiddling with the top button of my V-necked blouse and accidentally undid it, revealing my underwear. Can you imagine the tension of trying to look cool and credible, and at the same time do up the button again?

Women don't always err on the side of using body language that shows they are unsure of themselves. In an attempt to show that we're not nervous, we can also go over the top and appear cold and overpowering by holding ourselves rigidly and not smiling. Or nerves and insecurity can make us appear threatening rather than vulnerable.

> My training as a dancer made me stand very straight, and my northern background made me very direct. I would look people in the eye, stand tall and bluntly say what I thought. People assumed that I was very sure of myself. They found me particularly aggressive when I was disagreeing with them. Older people saw me as threatening and young people found me overwhelmingly confident. In fact I am quite introverted and shy. Until I learnt to moderate my body language I was treated quite harshly, because of the image I was putting across.

The best way to avoid these sort of situations is to practise deliberately using gestures and movements which not only show status, power and confidence but also warmth and friendliness. Let's look at each type of body language in turn to see how to project that desired image.

- *Eye contact* is critical in denoting status. High-status people look you in the eye; lower-status or unassertive people tend to avert their gaze. If you want to look confident, senior, open and trustworthy, look everyone in the eye. Don't look at the mouth and jaw, or at the forehead – because this won't do. Look them in the eye, but avoid a relentless stare. A socially-competent person will look briefly at your eyes when they start to speak, look away briefly, then back at you as they finish their point. A non-stop stare makes the other person uncomfortable and can even signal aggression.

• *Facial expression* An expressionless face is off-putting to most people, so you need to show some feeling as it makes you seem much more human. Also avoid anxious frowns or scowls of concentration. We do this more than we realise, especially when tense or stressed. I have heard it said that if a woman wants to look powerful and of high status she shouldn't smile, but I think that a warm confident smile at appropriate moments shows that you are relaxed and confident. In fact the more senior and powerful a woman is, the more she needs to smile. A successful woman *can* be an overpowering, intimidating figure. If you want to look feminine and approachable, as well as powerful, a smile will soften your image.

• *Posture* A person with a straight back, whether sitting or standing, looks as if she believes in herself. Also, stand with your weight evenly balanced on both feet. Swaying, standing on one leg and foot shuffling detract from poise. When sitting, rest your arms on the arms of the chair (if it's got arms) rather than crossing your arms over your chest. The latter denotes defensiveness. Try always to project an alert but relaxed image.

• *Gestures and mannerisms* are acceptable in moderation – always avoid gestures which denote girlishness or anxiety. But some gestures and hand movements can give positive messages of liveliness and enthusiasm, so don't rule them out altogether. Many of the gestures which involve touching our ears or noses or other parts of our face denote nervousness and should be avoided. Too much movement, jangling jewellery or keys are all distracting and detract from your poise. Certainly avoid excessive hand movements. People who wave their hands in the air with every point they make detract from their power and status, whether male or female.

Sitting in a calm, relaxed but attentive way is difficult if you are feeling tense or jittery because it is the excess nervous energy which causes us to fidget and twitch. But if you become aware of your own fidgeting and deliberately *act* as if you are calm and in control, it will actually make you feel less tense, reducing the need for excessive gestures.

Touching is a difficult subject in our culture and mostly we avoid touch with strangers as being too intimate. Women who are more inclined to touch can seem threatening or confusing. I am very put off by women who give hugs and kisses when I only know them in a work context. On the other hand, touching can produce an atmosphere of warmth and friendliness. I think the answer is to touch only in culturally acceptable ways if you don't know someone intimately. A warm handshake is best.

● *Voice* To appear powerful and assertive, we need strong clear voices which everyone can hear. Many women speak too softly which makes them seem unassertive, but a voice specialist can suggest exercises to resolve that problem. For most of us it is psychological, not physical. Ask you friends at work to tell you if you speak too softly; many women don't realise that they do.

● *Humour* The most important thing of all, is to be sufficiently relaxed and to be *humorous*. We women take ourselves so seriously! Life is full of situations that are ironic, farcical or just downright funny, but we are often trying so hard to get it right that we don't see the joke. So we're less fun to be with. Smiling, laughing and making humorous comments, in moderation, can all enhance your image. They can make you seem as if you're sufficiently on top of things to be relaxed.

SEXUAL ATTRACTION
One of the problems with body language is that there is a very fine dividing line between behaviour which signals interest and friendliness, and behaviour which signals sexual attraction. The signals which show you are sexually attracted to a man include:

● Smiling frequently
● A happy face
● Looking into his eyes
● Moving towards him
● Sitting facing him
● Touching his hand.

Now some of these behaviours – like smiling, eye contact and sitting facing him – are all appropriate to building rapport and developing a good working relationship. The question is, will this body language be mistaken for a sexual invitation? It is one of the problems women have to face up to. Body language is open to misinterpretation, and one of the factors is the receptiveness of the man you are talking to. If he is available, interested and self-confident, he may take your signals as a 'come on'. Wearing a wedding ring is no protection these days. But we do have some degree of control over the messages we give out although much of sex appeal is unconscious behaviour.

The thoughts you are thinking do colour the way you behave. If you are feeling attracted and available, the chances are you will signal it. This doesn't mean that you have to stifle your sexuality and guard against liking any man you meet at work, but it does mean that when you do feel attracted to a man you want to influence, you need to remind yourself that now is not the appropriate time to develop a personal relationship. Your body language should signal liking and interest, but nothing more.

However hard you try to avoid signalling sexual invitation, mistakes will be made. Men will ask you out, make flattering or suggestive personal remarks, or, at the least, call you 'dear' or 'love'. The question is how to deal with this when it happens, in a way that maintains your status and dignity, and without putting the other person down, especially in public?

Start off by ignoring the innuendos, the invitations and the 'dears'. Mostly these remarks are not meant to be offensive, so just change the subject. Unless your would-be suitor is really pressing or offensive, do not make an issue of it when it first happens. Instead try to build up your credibility by being very professional and establishing a good working relationship with the man in question. If it persists, then try to deal with it humorously. A light comment such as, 'You make me feel ten years old when you call me "dear", you know – I'd prefer it if you didn't,' will go down much better than, 'I must ask you to stop calling me "dear", I really don't like it.' If you can't think of something funny to say, just ask them to stop and say how it makes you feel, 'I wish you would stop asking me out, it makes me feel uncomfortable.' Once they realise that such attentions are not having the desired affect they will usually not want to carry on.

If the situation does get nasty and threatening, don't continue to try to deal with it on your own. Get help from whoever you feel safe to talk to: colleagues, personnel or other senior people. My advice about keeping it light only applies to cases that are not seriously threatening.

VARY YOUR BODY LANGUAGE

The more you become aware of your body language the more you can use it to signal a variety of messages. Obviously you want to look composed and poised, but you don't want to find yourself constrained by maintaining a rigid stance all the time, or acting a role. Be yourself, but in an acceptable way.

When a man is signalling dominance (or intimacy) by coming too close and invading your space, assert your own power by leaning back or stepping back and not smiling. You can also reassert your power with a confident eyeball-to-eyeball gaze – without scowling.

If on the other hand you want to show, in a conversation, that you are involved and interested in a particular point, lean forward slightly and allow your face to show animation. The occasional movement forward in this way punctuates the atmosphere with your energy. If you lean back and look composed all the time you may begin to appear too detached. On the other hand, sitting back and looking relaxed, accompanied by a warm smile and occasional nods of agreement can encourage the other person to open up.

When I am giving a presentation, if I continue standing and looking very self-confident when I ask the audience for questions, I usually don't get any. This is probably because I'm continuing to look dominant and assertive, and this encourages the audience to listen passively rather than discuss. If, on the other hand, I sit down, relax, smile cheerfully and invite questions, I always get them.

Dress

The main point about choosing appropriate and attractive clothes is that if you don't think you're good at it you can get some professional help. It will save you money in the end and will also help you to improve your image in a way that reflects your personality and lifestyle. If you want to get to the top, or even to the next rung, you have got to dress and behave as if you belong there.

Think big. When you have decided where you want to go and what sort of person you want to become, start acting and dressing as if you were there already. This will shorten your journey and make it more likely that you get where you want to go. We often understate our status and worth through poor image management. We need to begin to see clothes and body language as a legitimate vehicle for increasing our influence and making us more effective at work.

COLOUR

You need to find a way of projecting your femininity in smart, tailored clothes. The main route to achieving this is through colour and jewellery. Even a very tailored suit can look feminine if it's in a shade that suits you, worn with an attractive, colourful blouse and finished off with jewellery or a scarf. A dark suit does look very smart and gives an air of authority. Within the general advice from successful women to look tailored with feminine touches, was the message that you also have to look for clothes that suit your personality. Colour analysts are a great help to a business woman as they guide you towards those colours and shades that flatter your skin tones and make you stand out. (There are several good books on how to use colour effectively.)

The advice the colour analysts give is not to worry too much about your figure faults but to make the best of yourself with colours and styles that suit you. They can help you to identify the styles that flatter your particular figure and match your personality. Don't fall into the trap of thinking 'Oh, I'm too fat, thin, spotty, tired-looking, etc to do anything about my appearance just now.' This is a formula only for wasting valuable time. You can make the best of yourself and look good whatever your figure type, as long as you know what suits you or are prepared to take expert advice.

Colour analysts can help you to plan your wardrobe and accessories so that you minimise your spending on clothes by having jackets, bags, shoes and coats in one or other of the neutral colours that suit you. If you then stick to your best colours for your other clothes, the neutral colours will go with everything.

When you're travelling, having clothes that co-ordinate can really cut down on the luggage. You can go away for several days with one jacket, one skirt, one pair of shoes and three blouses. Just by changing your blouse and belt in the evening you can transform an outfit, although you may need to pack a travelling iron if your clothes crush.

You may want to have fun clothes for parties and weekends, but a limited wardrobe is all you need for work if you learn how to stick to your colours and mix and match.

Jennifer Rosenberg has some advice for women who want to look smart on limited budgets:

> You don't really need to buy suits. If you know what suits you, you can look good on very little money. One designer jacket, two skirts, a variety of tops and one or two good belts can give you five different outfits. To complete the image buy good shoes and handbags and keep them polished so that they last longer.

When I interviewed Jennifer she was wearing a blouse and skirt accessorised by a pair of high-heeled shoes, a lovely belt and some simple jewellery. She looked wonderful. She says she doesn't mind how often she wears an outfit, if she feels good in it. Her advice about accessories is also sound: good shoes and handbags do more to improve your image than most people realise. They do not need to be fabulously expensive, but they do need to be polished and flawless. Scuffed, worn accessories detract from the smartest outfit.

With leather items either buy expensive ones and keep them polished and make them last a long time, or buy less expensive ones and replace them as soon as they begin to show signs of wear. Jewellery can be costume, but it needs to be of reasonable quality. I have only one necklace and bracelet but they go with everything because they are gold.

If you want to look smart, everything about you needs to look the part. You've got to get the detail right.

MAKE-UP

The main advantage of make-up is that you look more finished, and you also look better. Women are often intimidated by make-up, and resist wearing it. But make-up is about putting the best *you* forward. Again colour analysts can come to your rescue and show you which shades and colours best suit your particular colouring. They can show you how to use make-up to highlight the best features of your face, whether that be high cheekbones or lovely eyes.

HAIR
Whether you like your hair long and curly, short and punky, or straight and sleek, or any other variation, it needs to be well cut and to have a distinct style. It is helpful to your image to have a well-cared for head of hair in a style that suits you.

Managing your image is not about trying to be something that you are not. It's about becoming aware of all your strengths, and using body language and dress to make the best of them. It's about being yourself and putting the best *you* forward – a you that makes a favourable impression on the rest of the world. Remember, if you look good, you'll look credible. Not only will other people believe in you, you will believe in yourself and your confidence will increase.

6

Interviews

In researching this chapter I spoke to a number of women who had experience of interviews, both at the giving and receiving end. I talked to people in personnel, and to headhunters and senior managers. As I did so a pattern began to emerge. Low self image and disinclination to plan careers are still holding women back from applying for top jobs. Also, when we go for interviews, we still tend to perform less well than men. In a world which has woken up to the fact that women are suitable applicants for a number of jobs, many managers and personnel officers would be pleased to select women for jobs which they would not have considered them for twenty years ago. Yet we are either not applying or are conducting ourselves at interviews in such a way that we obscure the strengths and personal qualities that we have to offer.

Interviews are important events for anyone hoping to do well in their career. Even if you are very good, you must convince your interviewer that you are, or you won't get the job or the promotion. If women tend to do poorly at interviews then that is yet another reason for the small number of women in senior appointments. Learning how to shine at interviews is as important to your career progress as is learning how to do your job well. In fact it can be even more important.

TAKE COURAGE AND APPLY FOR THE TOP JOBS
The headhunters I spoke to all had the same thing to say about women applying for senior and higher middle-grade jobs: they don't. The number of women applying for these jobs is never more than 10 per cent, and it is usually lower. The jobs most popular with women applicants are in television or financial management where the percentage of female applicants may be up to 10 per cent. For jobs in management or industry only 1 or 2 per cent of applicants are female. So very few of the 4.2 million working women in Britain apply for top posts.[10]

There are still people who say to the headhunters, 'We don't want a woman for this job.' Any reputable selection specialist will ignore that statement because it is against the law, but it does make it extremely unlikely that a woman will be chosen when there is that sort of prejudice.

The major obstacle to women being selected for senior jobs is that women don't apply for them. This is a shame, but in a way it is also encouraging, because it means that it is in our hands to do something about it.

Also encouraging is the fact that some senior managers and headhunters feel that, in many cases, the attributes they are looking for in these senior appointments are more likely to found in women than in men. Facilities management is a prime example of an area at which women are often more successful than men. A facilities manager is responsible for arranging office accommodation, and ensuring that these premises have the necessary services, such as telephones, computer terminals etc. It is a demanding job in which you are expected to carry out a huge variety of tasks, be in several places at the same time, and please everyone all of the time – which can't be done! It calls for tact, diplomacy and persuasiveness, and someone who is easygoing, immune to pressure and never panics. Often a man who feels he has to be dominant and confrontational will do this job less well than a woman.

In the race for the top, men are willing to apply for jobs that pay considerably more than they are currently earning but women don't have this confidence. Men will also apply for a job if they know they possess only some, not all, of the advertised criteria.

This way they at least give themselves the chance of making it. If you have some of the key qualities or experience that the selectors are looking for, and you impress them, they may be willing to take you on and either remould the job to fit you or train you in the skills you lack. Women rarely put themselves in a position to have this sort of good fortune because they do not usually apply unless they possess *all* the skills and qualities the advertisement asks for.

The first step in opening up opportunities is to apply for top jobs. Of course, just applying is not enough. Going for interviews is part of a career development package, which includes knowing where you want to go and what you want out of your next job, being prepared for the interview and knowing how to shine at that interview, and knowing how to evaluate the offers when they come. But you will probably not do these things if you don't first of all see yourself as someone who might be selected for these appointments. These jobs which can be either higher ranking positions in your present organisation or they can involve going to work for someone else.

BE YOURSELF AND BUILD A RELATIONSHIP WITH THE INTERVIEWER

The news from selection professionals about the performance of women at interviews is interesting. Progress has been made since the days when women were either too timid to say much, or blatantly tried to use their sex appeal to get jobs that needed other qualities! Women who go for junior or research jobs may still be too shy and quiet to give the interviewer a chance to find out enough about them. But women applying for middle and senior jobs have learnt to look confident and show that they are capable. The problem seems to be that they overdo it.

The career conscious woman tries much too hard to demonstrate that she is confident, efficient, capable, secure, in control, not at all nervous and not put out by being at an interview. The result of all this effort to look natural, relaxed and in charge is that they look anything but. They are clearly playing a part rather than being themselves and their performance is stilted. The outward signs of this tension over the effort to be natural is not quite knowing what to do with their hands, legs tightly crossed, with the knees and knuckles white. Women who try so hard to play a part at their interviews miss out on the most important thing that they should be doing, which is building rapport with the interviewer. They don't smile, don't make open gestures, don't chat about things and don't make comforting statements. Women tend to want to get down to business, and are not inclined to chat about themselves and build up a relationship with the interviewer.

Men are normally much easier to interview than women because they give you lots of anecdotes to illustrate their answers to questions, so it's not so difficult to get a good impression of what they are really like. Men use their charm to build rapport, whereas women repress the charm that they would normally use in a social situation. They just try to give you the facts, bang bang, with no anecdotes and no chat. The net effect is that these women seem rather cold, and it's difficult to find out enough about them to decide whether you want to give them the job. Coldness is the main reason why women are rejected for jobs. Nobody will give a job to a person they don't like!'

It's not difficult to understand why we make these mistakes. It's probably a reaction against how things used to be, where women were only promoted if they were exceptionally capable spinsters who were prepared to sacrifice everything for their careers, or manipulative enough to use their sex appeal to get what they wanted. There used to be a myth that sexy women who were free with their favours got on better in their careers. I don't know if this ever was true, but the case now seems to be that men are rather put off by a woman who blatantly flouts her sexuality at an interview. The following tale was told by a male interviewer.

I interviewed a woman once who could only be called a vamp. She was very well endowed anyway, but she didn't leave it at that. She wore false eyelashes and played the part of a 'femme fatale'. She spent the interview trying to impress me with her womanly charms. It was awful; I just wanted to escape. I was interviewing her for a job at Fords. Her final mistake was to say breathlessly, 'I have always wanted to meet a man from Shell.'

Most of us know that this sort of approach doesn't work but now we seem to be going too far in the other direction. In our attempt to avoid being seen as sex objects we are throwing the baby out with the bath water. Using charm, warmth and openness are not only ways of attracting a man sexually, they are appropriate as a means of building a working relationship too. And don't forget that it's equally important to be warm and charming to female interviewers. They are human too!

DEALING WITH NERVES

If you are too nervous to be your usual warm, friendly, charming self, then this will obviously be a problem. Preparing for the interview and planning how to answer difficult questions will help enormously to increase your confidence. I deal with this later in the chapter. But if you're still feeling jittery while you're sitting in the waiting room, try taking some slow, deep breaths – filling your lungs with oxygen has a surprisingly calming effect. Try to see the interviewer as a human being who is probably going to try to help you to perform at your best. They may be feeling nervous as well.

THE RULES OF THE GAME

Interviews are a game, and to play it well you must learn the rules. Hesitations, speech errors, speaking too quickly and looking timid will give the message that you are lacking in power and stature for a senior job. But being super-confident and super-efficient can also lose you the game. The trick is to go to an interview with the attitude that you are going to have a friendly, open conversation with an *equal*, even if your interviewer is the chairman of the largest company in Europe. Go prepared to work together with the interviewer so that you can both decide whether you are right for that job, and whether the job is right for you. To liaise with someone over such an important decision you have got to build up a good working relationship quickly.

Use some charm and warmth, chat about yourself, ask her (or him) questions and smile or laugh at appropriate times. Try not to put them off by being too intense, serious and clipped. You have got to show them that you are a nice person whom they will enjoy working with, as well as being someone with the experience to carry out the job. Put yourself in the interviewer's shoes and try to imagine how boring it can be to have interview after interview with bland, serious people, all playing a part. Being yourself, showing warmth, and having a rapport with the interviewer will make *you* the memorable, impressive candidate.

One senior woman demonstrated this with an interesting tale of one of her experiences as a candidate. She only discovered that the job was on offer five weeks after the cut-off date for applications, but telephoned the company anyway and asked for an interview.

'Oh we can't see you now,' they said, 'We have finished interviewing and have drawn up a shortlist.'

'But I'm only just round the corner,' replied this woman. 'I can be with you within minutes.'

They finally agreed to interview her and in the middle of it they said, 'We'll have to confess that, good though you are, we were really looking for a chap. This is a very male-oriented organisation. The other staff are all men.'

'Well,' she said, undeterred, 'I can wear a suit and tie, and speak in a low voice, but I can't grow a beard.'

She got the job.

Interviews should be two-way affairs. If you ask some of the questions and do some of the assessing, then it may help to take the pressure off, to lessen that feeling that you are a tame performing monkey.

However, the pattern that emerges when talking to interviewers is that women don't ask probing questions about the job, and they are often not clear about what sort of post they are looking for. This is in line with our tendency to avoid career planning and setting career goals. One experienced interviewer put it this way:

Women don't research themselves before they research the job, so they don't analyse what they want the job for. They expect the interviewer to be psychic and to know what they want in a job. You need to find out things like: the management style in the organisation, what is expected of you and how your performance is going to be measured. For example, are you going to be judged by your strategy, or just on the bottom line? If you are clear about what sort of person you are and what you are looking for in the job, then you can evaluate what you discover about the organisation at the interview. You must be alert. You've got to smell the organisation from the front door in. Does it look sloppy, busy, or frantic? Do the staff look like the sort of people you would want to spend your time with? Sometimes women see at the interview stage that the job looks too difficult and demanding because of the attitudes or set-up in the organisation, yet they still accept the job. Don't accept the impossible; you might think you can push water uphill but you can't.

Other women spoke of their experiences in preparing for job hunting and interviews.

You need to work out what you want from both the job and for your life in terms of the culture and the environment. When you find out what the company is like, ask yourself – can I be me, or can I be the me that I want to become in this organisation? When I was applying for my present job I wanted something very different from being a director in a large manufacturing company. I wanted to work for a smaller company which was relatively new so that I could help in building it up. I wanted to move away from manufacturing to the service sector and I wanted a job that was intellectually stretching. If you've done this sort of preparation then you're much more impressive at the interview.

I spend some time considering what sorts of companies are the best ones to apply to. I've decided that you shouldn't try to fight everything at once. For example, if you're trying to change your job function, get a more senior post *and* a higher income, that's probably enough to be getting on with. So if you look for organisations who are used to having women at management level then at least you won't have to fight that battle as well. With this in mind I applied to computer companies and accountancy companies who do tend to have women managers. I also applied to big prestigious companies because I was at a stage in my career when I needed to add some big names to my CV. You really need to have a clear line on what you want the job to achieve for you.

Do this kind of thinking *before* you go to an interview. Don't just think about what you can do to impress the interviewer. Work out what you want from the job and use the opportunity to discover whether it offers what you need at this stage in your career. Remember, for most middle or senior jobs the majority of candidates will be male. Interviewers will be accustomed, therefore, to dealing with people who have a vision of where they are going and who have worked out their career goals. If you show that you haven't thought beyond next year, and that you don't know what you are aiming for or what you want the job to do for you, then you will be taken less seriously than the competition.

Most interviewers expect and want you to ask them about how the job fits in with your career needs, and they will therefore be surprised and disappointed if you have no questions to put to them.

It's very bad if you do not have any questions to ask at the end of the interview when you are invited to ask about the job. Sometimes people who do have questions are so nervous that they forget what they wanted to ask. To prevent this happening, plan a few questions beforehand and write them on a note pad which you bring with you. Your interviewer will be impressed with your planning and preparation if you take out this pad at the appropriate time. If you really get stuck then say that you had lots of questions but they were all answered during the course of the interview. If you want the job you must show that you're interested in the organisation and how you could fit into it.

Don't be afraid to ask questions and to negotiate about your salary and job title. The male candidates will do this, but women are notoriously bad at discussing these things. They tend to avoid the subject and end up just accepting what they are offered. The best time for these points is normally at the second interview, after you have been shortlisted. You also need to clarify whether the job gives you as much authority as you want and need. I know someone who recently left a well-paid job a few months after starting because, contrary to her assumptions, all the decisions were made by her boss, leaving her to follow orders. This is the sort of detail you need to ask about in the interview, not after you've started work!

Deciding where you want to go and what you want out of the job, is only half of the preparation needed for an interview. The other half is to research the organisation you're being interviewed for. You will not be expected to have all the information about the company at your fingertips, but you should know the key facts.

You should have read the brochure and know the size of the company and the products or services it supplies. If you are applying for a professional job you should know what the relevant qualifications are and should have thought through the implications of studying for the exams if you're not already qualified.

Sometimes the company or the industry or service had been in the news lately, in which case you should be aware of what is going on. For instance, if you knew nothing about a recent strike or disaster which affected the company you would probably not be considered for the job. If the unions are a significant factor in the company or industry, you should know this. (Sometimes, being a member of that union – or being prepared to become a member – may be very relevant to your chances.) One candidate applying for a post in a television company knew nothing about unions in television. She did not get the job. Another candidate applying for a job on a magazine confessed to having only briefly looked at the magazine for the first time the day before and therefore knew little about it. She was not successful either.

Why do you need to do this research? For two reasons. Firstly, the interviewer wants to make sure that you are not embarking on a job or a career which would not suit you. If you show ignorance of the company you have clearly not thought through whether a job with them is really what you want. Secondly, this is another way of testing whether you are motivated enough about your career to have done some planning and research.

If you find it difficult to think on your feet and sometimes go blank under pressure in an interview, don't feel badly about it. Many senior people confess to having had experiences like this. If this does happen to you, then learn how to anticipate the problem and prevent it recurring, like these women have done.

> When I am preparing for an interview I try to work out what they are likely to ask me. I then think through answers to these questions so that I don't get caught out with nothing to say. The sort of questions that I need to plan ahead for are ones like
>
> Why do you want this job?
> What are your strengths and weaknesses?
>
> If it's an internal job I try to find out who else is being interviewed and get an idea from them of what sorts of questions are being asked.

'Tell me about your strengths,' seems to be a popular request at interviews. Some of the women I spoke to don't like being asked this, but have learnt that having a glib answer or no answer at all doesn't do them much good.

When I was asked, 'What are your greatest strengths?' I said, 'I'm very bright'. To 'What are your greatest weaknesses?' I replied, 'Chocolates'. They *are* my greatest weakness, but I didn't get the job!

Once I was asked to tell the interviewer my strengths. I said I was creative. When he said, 'How are you creative?' I froze. I just couldn't think of any examples. Now I have learnt to prepare for questions like that and I think about the follow through and go armed with some examples. The sort of questions that I prepare for are the 'how do you deal with' ones. For example – how do you deal with: stress, ambiguity, pressure, people and travel. I also have to think through what my multinational experiences have been because it's the multinationals I am applying to at present.

Other questions that come up frequently at interviews are:

'Why are you thinking of leaving your present job?'
'Tell me a bit about yourself.'
'Why do you want to work for us?'

It's very hard to answer these on the spot if you haven't thought the answers through beforehand. When asked why you are leaving your present job, do resist the temptation to run your employers down. This is never well received. Try to find something positive and forward-looking to say about your decision. Instead of saying,

I'm leaving because it's an awful place to work. My boss is a really bitchy woman who doesn't like me and I'm sure I'll never get a promotion from her.

Try:

I'm looking for an opportunity to do more responsible work.

There doesn't seem much chance of a promotion in my present job, so I've decided to look outside.

To prepare for the question 'Tell me a bit about yourself', try to think of the facts about you, your interests and your career which are relevant to the job you are applying for. An answer like this would do the trick:

I am twenty-nine years old, I love the sort of work I do and I am very ambitious. I am fairly outgoing and I like jobs that involve dealing with other people. I am not a loner and am unhappy if I have to spend too much time on my own . . .

If you have done your homework and have found out all you can about the organisation, then you should be able to answer the question, 'Why do you want to work for us?' If you are only partly attracted to the job you don't need to lie. Say what you like about the organisation, and express concern or ask questions about those aspects you think you may not like. The interviewer will respect you if you know what you want and are genuinely trying to discover if the job meets your needs.

If you turn up for the interview armed with career plans, knowledge about the company, questions to ask the interviewer and answers to difficult ones they might ask you, this should help you to feel more confident.

The next thing to think about is how to manage your image in the interview so that you get the most out of it. I have already mentioned the need to be natural and to show your real self, but you might find the following tips on dress and behaviour helpful.

EFFECTIVE DRESS AND BEHAVIOUR
All the points I covered in Chapter 5, on managing your image, will be helpful at an interview. But it's worth elaborating on dress and behaviour here so that you learn to avoid some common mistakes women make at interviews.

The main point to think about is that most interviewers make up their minds in the first few minutes whether you're in with a chance or not. That's how powerful first impressions are. You may not be able to clinch the job in the first five minutes, but you certainly can disqualify yourself. Remember, it is important to the whole process to get started on the right foot. If you succeed, you've got a chance to influence the other person; if you fail, you're wasting your time – they have already decided that they won't give you a chance. The same thing happens at an interview. So try to avoid disqualifying yourself at the start with dress or behaviour that puts the interviewer off.

Even if the interviewer is trying hard to be fair, everything you say later on will be coloured by the initial impression you have made. This process is called the 'halo' and 'horn' effect. If you've made a good first impression the 'halo' effect operates and the interviewer will make allowances for you, and see potential wherever possible. If your first impression is poor, then watch out for the 'horn' effect because the interviewer will judge you harshly and look for weaknesses rather than promise.

Dress is important at an interview just because first impressions are *so* decisive. If your appearance puts someone off you may never get a chance to prove that you are worth your weight in gold. Some women do look very chic when they turn up for interviews, but many more get it wrong. Power dressing can make you look too clinical, so soften tailored suits with blouses in flattering colours and with tasteful jewellery. The other way of getting it wrong is to dress too casually, or not to pay enough attention to detail. If you look scruffy or dowdy you will probably not be considered for a senior appointment or one where your image is important because you need to impress other people. Don't let your dress deny you the chance to be selected.

You don't need to wear expensive clothes, but you do need to get the detail right and to look well groomed. Some interviewers said that they were always noticing things like dirty fingernails, bra straps falling down, petticoats showing, laddered tights and scuffed shoes.

Hair also needs to be thought about. If it's scraped back it can make you look too severe. If it's very untidy or badly cut you won't look well-groomed. Some sort of compromise that makes you look feminine and your hair look cared for will give the right message.

Interviewers also mentioned that they were distracted and put off by bangles jangling, bags rattling and keys put on the table. The worst thing you can do is to walk into the interview with shopping bags or carriers full of food. Men apparently do this quite often as well! If you have shopping bags with you, ask the receptionist or the secretary to keep them for you so that you don't give an unfavourable impression when you meet the interviewer.

When you walk into the interview room behave as if you are pleased and interested to be there. Smile at the interviewer, shake her or his hand, and react in a warm, friendly way that is natural to *you*. Don't try to play a part or to be someone you are not. Sit down and put your handbag on the floor beside you. If the chair puts you in an awkward position, then get up and move it and say why you're doing so. It will help you to seem at ease and as if you are in control of the situation.

FIRST IMPRESSIONS

Candidates often don't realise that they are under scrutiny from the moment they walk in through the front door. I was told a sad story about a woman who was the best-qualified person for a senior job. However, when she came for her second interview she made a bad mistake *outside* the interview room. She arrived on time but there was no one at reception . . . finally, as the time ticked away, she became fearful that her interviewer might be waiting for her upstairs and think that she was late. She then marched into a nearby office where she found a few junior staff to whom she explained the situation and asked to be announced. But she was very abrupt with them and turned on her heel and walked back to reception when she had said her piece. As it turned out, had she got the job she would have been supervising these people. Later, they commented on her rudeness to the interviewer and she did not get the job. Her rudeness stemmed from her nervousness, of course, but it was unfortunate. You need to show you are human and pleasant to everyone, not just the person doing the selecting. Sometimes candidates are offensive to headhunters and selection professionals, not realising that if they aren't nice to these people they won't be put forward for the job.

When it comes to managing your image through your behaviour, charm, femininity and naturalness are the key words. There is only one rule which I think we should all pay attention to and that is to look the interviewer in the eye. If you are very nervous the interviewer will understand if you look down at first, while you are settling in. Most interviewers realise that interviews can be stressful and they are usually struggling themselves to find ways of putting you at ease. If, however, you never settle down and you never look at the interviewer, you might as well write off the job. Nobody wants to employ a person who won't look them in the eye.

There are things you can do to help you be more confident at the interview, and more able to be yourself. I have already mentioned the advantages of career planning, research and preparing answers to difficult questions. If you feel well prepared for an interview it will help you feel less nervous. There are other simpler things you can do to prevent disaster and to calm your nerves, as you will see:

Always make sure a few days before that the clothes you are planning to wear are clean and ready. Bring a spare pair of tights. Always go to the lavatory before the interview starts. Nerves can play havoc with your bladder!

The most important lesson I have learnt is to arrive in plenty of time. I remember going for my first interview with my mother who came along to give support and help me find my way. We didn't leave any extra time for the journey and sure enough the bus was diverted and instead of taking us to the building went off down a side street to a part of the city we didn't know. We got off the bus, not knowing where we were, with ten minutes to spare and in a panic. Somehow we separated in an effort to discover where we were and how to get a bus back to the right place. I then saw a taxi and was in such a rush that I got in and told them to take me to the interview address. I went off leaving my poor mother down the road looking for the right bus! I arrived at the interview with no time to spare and feeling very flustered and rather guilty. It was very hard to perform effectively for the first half of the interview!

Leaving the interview is as important as entering. Say goodbye in a friendly way and shake hands, looking the interviewer in the eye. If in your nervousness you make the classic boob of spilling the contents of your handbag all over the floor then take heart from the fact that you are not the first person to have done this. Make a joke of it and don't get too flustered and apologetic. If you handle awkward situations well you can turn a potential disaster to your advantage.

PANEL INTERVIEWS

For some jobs you will be interviewed by a panel of people. Usually such panels are small, say three interviewers, but even this number can be more intimidating than a one-to-one interview. The interviewers will usually take turns to ask questions, and the best way to handle it is to look at the person who is doing the questioning. Concentrate on the questioner and look them in the eye, then when someone else takes over, turn your attention to them. This will make it easier for you, and increases your chances of building up your relationship with each person on the panel.

HELP THE INTERVIEWER TO DISCOVER *ALL* YOUR STRENGTHS AND QUALITIES

The interviewer is trying to get as much information about you as possible so that he or she can make a good decision. You may be very suitable for the job, but if the interviewer doesn't get to find this out in the interview, you won't be selected. There are several ways of inadvertently misleading the interviewer, or of obscuring useful information about yourself. Some of these ways I have discussed already – like playing a role and giving a stilted performance or giving the wrong impression by dressing inappropriately.

One of the methods that a trained interviewer will use to learn what sort of person you are is to ask you open questions to get you talking, and home in with direct probing questions when you say something they want more factual information on. The process might go like this.

INTERVIEWER (open question) 'Tell me something about your management duties in your present job.'

CANDIDATE 'I have ten staff, seven of whom are salesmen and three are administrative. I am responsible for motivating the sales team, ensuring that they set realistic targets and achieve them. It can be quite a problem just keeping in touch with them because they have to do so much travelling. I have to plan meetings at least a month in advance to get them all to attend.'

INTERVIEWER (direct probing question) 'What methods do you use to motivate the sales team?'

It is very important that you give full answers to these open questions so that the interviewer can get a picture of your skills, experience and approach to work. According to the personnel specialists I spoke to, women are not as good as men at answering open questions. We tend to give the shortest possible reply and do not develop the theme. This gives the interviewer a problem because we aren't providing enough information about ourselves. The interview then proceeds more like an interrogation than like a conversation with the interviewee doing most of the talking, which is how it should be.

The interviewer will usually have a list of the skills, qualities and experience we need to demonstrate that we have in order to get the job. Later in this chapter I will give you an idea of the sorts of skills and qualities they will be looking for in different types of work. The point is that if you don't give them full enough, or relevant, answers to their questions, they won't be able to decide if you have what they are looking for. We can make this mistake either because we are too shy or nervous to say much, or because we are trying too hard to show our efficiency and give short, clipped answers to everything. Another mistake we can make is to give irrelevant answers in our attempt to be chatty and conversational. Here is an example.

INTERVIEWER (open question) 'Tell me about your present job.'

CANDIDATE 'There were six of us in the office and we had to get all the information ready for head office on the sales figures each week. This meant going to each department by the Thursday and getting them to fill in the pink forms and the blue forms. The pink forms asked for figures on . . .'

This candidate is making the mistake of telling the interviewer lots of boring detail about the job, but nothing about *her*. The interviewer only wants a brief idea of the tasks, but lots of information about how *you* approach these tasks, and what skills *you* have to use. A much more valuable answer would have been:

My task was getting information on sales figures out of the departments each week. We were working to deadline so not only did I have to cope with that pressure, but I had to persuade the staff in each department to produce their data on time. This required a lot of tact and persistence as they were always overworked and wanted to put my information aside.

Again if you spend too much time on irrelevancies the interviewer may not discover enough about your skills and experience to feel safe in offering you the job. Another method interviewers will use to find out more about you is to ask you what you do in your leisure time. Here they are trying to discover things like:

- Whether you are a loner or like team activities.
- Whether you are an energetic, enthusiastic person.
- Whether you use your organisational or leadership skills in any of your leisure activities.
- Any relevant personality attributes like perseverance, creativity, patience, endeavour etc.

Unfortunately, many candidates don't see the point of these questions and may hide all sorts of sterling qualities by giving short, meaningless answers. Professional interviewers say that women in particular give unhelpful replies here – they give no feeling of what they really love doing and instead give the answers they think the interviewer is looking for. Men, on the other hand, are better at showing that they really enjoy themselves at some of their leisure activities, and reveal much more about their personalities.

Don't worry if your leisure activities don't sound intellectual or noble. The interviewer simply wouldn't believe it if all the candidates said they liked reading Proust and served on the church committee! If you spend your evenings going to discos and parties then say so, and also say how much you enjoy them. You might then give the impression that you are a sociable, well-balanced person and this could be in your favour.

When you are answering questions in an interview you should not take them at face value. You need to remember that the interviewer is looking for information about you and you've got to try to work out how you can demonstrate your skills, experience and qualities by the way you answer.

Many interviewers will ask you quite blatantly sexist questions like:

How will you manage your family and work such long hours?

How will you, as an attractive woman, cope with advances from male customers?

How will your husband feel about you travelling around the country with other men, and spending so much time away from home?

It doesn't help to point out that these questions are against the law! If you do have a family, tell the interviewer how you manage the situation in a matter-of-fact, down-to-earth way. I always explain how my family life is managed even if I am not asked, because I feel by doing this I can demonstrate my organisational ability and planning skills. As for the other questions, I simply state calmly that I have learnt how to cope with the situation. Often women who have not yet had children are asked if they are planning to do so. One senior woman deals with that question well and says, 'I don't know, but if I do have children I *will* be returning to work.'

Sometimes these sexist questions are asked in quite a hostile way. If your interviewer is going to be your boss, you may need to consider whether you want to work for such a person. It could be an uphill struggle to get someone with such views to see you as an employee to be respected and promoted.

Sometimes interviewers try to find out how you respond to challenges by asking difficult questions or making controversial statements. If you agree with everything they say and back away from the challenge, they may assume that you don't know how to stand up for yourself, or don't hold any strong views. One of the women I spoke to had this experience to relate.

I was applying for a senior job and the interviewer said they felt the job was operational rather than strategic. I disagreed fundamentally with this and decided not to let it pass. I said politely that I thought that the operational aspects of the job ought to be linked with strategy. I don't know whether he was testing me or not, but he just nodded pleasantly and I got shortlisted.

This woman had the courage to speak up about her views, but she disagreed pleasantly and courteously and so made a favourable impression.

SELECTION CRITERIA

A useful part of your preparation before going to an interview will be to work out beforehand what sort of skills, experience and qualities will be most relevant to the job; in other words, what will be the *selection criteria*. Most interviewers work out their selection criteria beforehand, although some are more systematic about this than others. These criteria will be different for different jobs. I have chosen six types of job: In each case I spoke to interviewers who chose people for these jobs and they gave me an idea of the selection criteria.

● *Clerical officer* With clerical jobs the main questions are, can you cope with routine repetitive work, does this sort of job really interest you and can you work without being constantly supervised? Usually clerical jobs involve team work, so the interviewer will probe to see if you are tolerant of other people and have previous experience of working (or playing) with groups. They are trying to avoid employing people who will disrupt the office by working slowly or carelessly, by picking fights with others or by being insolent or sulky. They will also test to see whether you are versatile and flexible enough to cope with new technology.

The interviewer will be particularly interested in your previous employment history. They need to know what sorts of work you have done and what responsibilities you've had. They will probe statements on your application form like 'left for personal reasons' in case these personal reasons are still significant and could affect the job in question. If you are evasive they will assume you have something to hide. They will want to know if you have ever been dismissed and why. They will also want to know if you've had any long periods of unemployment and why. Again, if you are evasive they will assume the worst.

● *General administrator* This is quite a demanding post. The interviewer will be searching to see if you have the intellectual ability to cope and to develop ideas of your own. He or she will also want to see if you are a practical person and a good communicator. If the interviewer fails to engage you in a dialogue you won't be getting this job!

As far as personal qualities are concerned you will need to be warm, friendly and approachable, flexible, reliable and confident enough to see things through. The sorts of things that would put the interviewer off would be any sign of moodiness, poor listening, an abrasive manner, defensiveness or a tendency to lean too much towards one way of working.

● *Art teacher* With this job the question is, 'Do you have both the technical expertise and the ability to handle a class of school children?' Your ability to inspire a group of children and to hold their interest will be an important issue. You will need to demonstrate that you have the social skills and personality to relate to the children.

Learning in art is quite different from learning in more academic subjects. Art lessons are often seen as an opportunity for relaxation rather than for learning. You will need to show that you understand these difficulties and can handle the dilemmas they pose. More precisely, you may have to show you can:

1 Deal with the child who doesn't want to know about art, and thinks it's a load of rubbish.
2 Deal with children who think that speed is the most important aspect of learning and teach them how to slow down.
3 Get children to realise that art is about expressing themselves rather than about absorbing information.
4 Get children to realise that their own thoughts and feelings are valid and worthy of expression.

You will need to show what projects you would set to enable children to realise that they have the potential to express themselves creatively.

● *Accountant or Actuary* This interviewer selects candidates for a large financial company. She is mostly interviewing candidates for actuarial jobs, but the selection criteria would be equally valid for accountants.

Education is the biggest hurdle because passing the exams is difficult. The other criteria are motivation, appearance, leadership and teamwork.

The interviewer is looking for someone with the motivation to have this career, study for the exams, and work for this particular company. Candidates need to show that they have done some research so that they have the information to make these important career decisions. You need to have contacted the professional institutes to discover how long it normally takes to pass the exams and what subjects are on the syllabus. You will have to show that you have thought through how long it will take *you* to get through the exams and how you plan to structure your life around them (sport, children etc). You will be asked why you have chosen a financial company rather than a consultancy. You will also be expected to know about this particular organisation and explain why you are interested in working for them. The interviewer will be very keen to ensure that she does not select people who are accidentally choosing the wrong career.

Appearance is important. Are you going to fit in with the other people on the team? That is what the interviewer is worried about. So if someone turned up in jeans they would be thought stupid and naïve. Usually women wear suits and this is fine but there is no need to go over the top; in fact, it could make the interviewer feel uncomfortable. The interviewer is looking for a person, not a machine, so bland, boring, safe outfits are a mistake. The search is for a bit of individuality, someone who will add something of themselves to the job.

Leadership and teamwork are usually tested in group exercises. Women consistently do less well in these group exercises, probably because their voices are too soft. They find it hard to deal with domineering men who talk too much and ignore their perfectly sound proposals. In these group exercises your ability to influence the group in an assertive, acceptable way is what you need to demonstrate. People who behave in domineering, aggressive ways and who put other people down will not stand a good chance of being selected, but if you allow yourself to be squeezed out of the dialogue then you may not be chosen either. If you also find it difficult to speak up or to be heard in these often highly-competitive exercises, you won't give the impression that you can be assertive and influential. If you read the chapter on meetings before your next interview it should help to improve your performance in these rather difficult situations.

Any experience on committees, participation in team sports, and leadership positions in things like the Girl Guides or sports teams will be an advantage. Warning lights will ring for the interviewer if you lived in lodgings as a student rather than in hall, went home to your parents *every* holiday instead of going off with friends, and prefer activities like chess, war games and computer games to team games. They will assume you are a loner and that you won't be a good team member.

- *Training consultant* This job is for experienced trainers, not for graduates who want to start a training career. The criteria are therefore that much more demanding. Creativity, communication skills and the ability to handle concepts are the key criteria. The interviewer will expect you to be good at selling yourself. You will be expected to have read the job advertisement carefully and to relate whatever you have done that is relevant in every subject you have worked in and say what you have *learnt* from each experience. You will be expected to have your own views on a variety of different subjects. The interviewer will also be interested to see if you can handle criticism, not by being defensive, but by giving the underlying reason for what you are doing. They wouldn't expect you to be bothered unduly by criticism, or by a challenge, but to handle it assertively.

- *Chief executive* This is, of course, a very senior job and the criteria reflect that. Interestingly, even at this level, selectors are still looking for human beings rather than machines!

Your previous employment history needs to demonstrate that you have experience at senior level and at the relevant job functions. Usually interviewers are hoping to see experience from a variety of different appointments.

It is very important that you show that you can manage a team, because you can't possibly do everything yourself. You will need to demonstrate that you are good at letting people around you grow and develop. People who are insecure surround themselves with weak people and the interviewer will want to check that you are not one of these! You need to be able to acknowledge that there is excellence elsewhere and not spend the interview building yourself up and putting others down. The interviewer will be on guard against pomposity.

Your approach to projects and your job will be probed. Do you make things happen, or do things happen to you? Do you plan and prepare before acting? Do you take criticism personally or can you assess your mistakes objectively and learn from them? Do you focus on your job, or do you take on other people's responsibilities when you shouldn't? Are you up-to-date on current affairs and aware of how the environment affects you?

You will certainly be probed on your leisure activities. The selectors are not looking for a chief executive who wants to use the company as his or her social life. That sort of person doesn't bring outside cultures, experiences and contacts to enrich the organisation. You may also give the impression that you are insecure if you prefer to spend all your time with the company. Outside interests and commitments are a big bonus for a job like this, and any evidence of leadership roles in sports clubs or community activities will be a real advantage to you. Women should never apologise for family commitments. This can be seen as a plus, and evidence of planning and organisational skills. You will seem more emotionally healthy if you enjoy spending time with your children, more as if you have a lot to give.

You can often get an idea of some of the selection criteria by reading the job advertisement. You will need to ask any friends or contacts you have who work in the field for further ideas on what the selectors may be looking for. When you have put together your idea of the selection criteria for the post, work out how you can demonstrate, through your job history and your leisure activities, that you fulfil them. This will help you to give much more effective answers to the questions. In fact, even if you are unlucky and get a bad interviewer who has not planned the interview, if you have some idea of what he or she might be looking for you can provide the information anyway.

When you have worked out the selection criteria you may decide that you are not the right sort of person for the job and that you would not be happy there. This will save you a lot of time. On the other hand, if you have most of the criteria but not all, you may decide to go for it anyway. In the interview you can stress your relevant strengths, and say how you plan to develop in those areas in which you are weak. Remember, men don't worry about not fulfilling all the required criteria, so why should you? You might get the job anyway, if you are particularly strong in the main qualities needed.

The news is not all bad for women interviewees. Professional interviewers say that women are usually better at compiling CVs. In some fields like publishing, where lots of women are employed, the women candidates often perform better than the men. Women are less likely to be arrogant and pompous at interviews than men, or to try to put the interviewer down. But I think the most encouraging development of all is that selectors are generally much more inclined to consider female candidates than they were in the past. If we decide to plan our careers, imagine ourselves in senior jobs in areas where we have experience and apply for those posts, it will certainly improve our chances of doing well. If we add to this careful preparation before the interview, and the ability to be ourselves and show our charm and warmth at the interview, then the world could be our oyster!

7
Making an impact at a meeting

TO BE SILENT AT A MEETING IS TO BE INVISIBLE.

Meetings are critically important when you are trying to move up and on in an organisation, because they are opportunities to show other people how well you operate. You are assessed by your performance in meetings much more than by your day-to-day routine work and those who realise this have one of the keys to progress. This chapter shows why meetings are so important to a career woman. It points out the particular problems that hinder women from being effective in meetings, and explains what to do about them.

Many people find meetings difficult – they can be boring, frustrating, disorganised and ineffective. Under pressure to get their own way, or just to get in on the act, people can be quite nasty and aggressive to each other. It is normal in such situations to feel anxious, frightened, irritated or pressurised, and to show it. And even in a constructive, well-chaired meeting an inexperienced or shy person can feel overawed by the apparent confidence of the other participants and the pace of the decision making. It is also more difficult to be influential in a meeting than in an interview with just one other person. The fact that there are several people there, all with something to say, all with their own emotions – sometimes negative – and with varying personal objectives, makes it much more complicated. Quite often women feel turned off by the disorder and competition in a meeting, and simply give up the attempt to contribute. Yet meetings are so vital that we must learn how to cope with them.

Visibility at meetings

Meetings are shop windows in many different ways. For a relatively junior woman they are opportunities to meet senior people whom you do not see in the normal course of your work.

Judy Presnell has this all worked out, 'I've learnt to make myself very visible at meetings. Important people come to them, *and* people from other areas within the company. It may be the only situation in which high-powered people see me.'

The point is that these people will often be making decisions on your promotion, or on giving you responsible tasks that could lead to it. If you fail to impress them at meetings, then you've lost a good opportunity. They may even block your progress.

In my work as a consultant I got to know a woman manager in a large organisation who performed well and deserved a promotion. Her appraisals given by her immediate boss were good, but the promotion never came. When we discussed it further, I discovered that the promotion decision was made by her boss's boss, whom she saw only twice a year at meetings. Unfortunately, she did not perform well at these meetings because, inhibited by the presence of such a senior person, she said nothing most of the time and when she had to speak she did so hesitantly and got her ideas confused. The boss's boss therefore thought she was unassertive and not ready for a senior job.

Meetings are also shop windows for more senior women in another, less obviously important way. They are usually the only opportunities many of their junior staff will have to work with them. Senior women are still rarities and therefore the subject of much speculation and gossip, so meetings are occasions when you can show that you are human and approachable, as well as decisive and in control.

The behaviour of senior women, particularly at meetings,

presentations and social events, is noticed and analysed by every-one. I can think of one woman in particular who, in a markedly masculine environment, was an excellent manager, good at com-pany politics, superb at career planning and very fair with her staff. However, at meetings she was a disaster, everyone in her department complained about her behaviour there: she was loud, aggressive, argumentative and domineering. She wasted a lot of time and was very emotive and negative, making it difficult for others to speak or come to objective decisions. Her public image in the company was determined by her performance at meetings so she acquired a bad reputation. Unfortunately for her, her other good qualities were obscured by this. However, there are also senior women who enhance their reputation by being clear-thinking and assertive at meetings.

Meetings with people outside your company – suppliers, cus-tomers etc – are excellent opportunities to impress the business world at large. When you are looking for a new job these informal contacts can be valuable. If you are self employed or running your own business, most of your meetings will be with outsiders. In this position you depend heavily on your customers and suppliers, so skilful behaviour at meetings is essential for negotiating and growing.

INTERVENTIONS

Having established that meetings provide opportunities to show ourselves in a good light, let us examine why women tend not to sparkle on these occasions. It is a fact that having softer, higher-pitched voices than men is one obvious physical disadvantage. Assumptions about our low status provide another. Many people habitually ignore those who are soft-spoken or of low-status. Research indicates that in mixed company men do a higher proportion of the talking, and interrupt more.

Men also use wordy speeches to give themselves more 'air space', to get attention and to signal their status. This is a problem for women in meetings. We are generally better at identifying the core of the issue and avoiding waffle, but find it difficult getting into the conversation and staying there against male interrup-tions. If we try to use male tactics and talk a great deal and interrupt frequently, somehow that doesn't signal status in a woman, just aggression. Instead we have to be pleasantly assertive when we have something to say, and to courageously get back in there when we have been interrupted.

Try saying something like:

'Hold on, Jim, I wasn't quite through.'

Or,

'Just a minute, Peter, I've got a few more points to make on that topic.'

Or,

'Alastair, I just need another minute to finish that one off.'

Alternatively you can wait until your interrupter has finished and then quickly come in with a comment like this:

'Before we get too far down that road, let me finish what I was saying about oil paints.'

Our conditioning as women certainly does not help us at meetings. We are taught to defer to men and this makes it harder to stand up to them in public. We have not learnt how to do it in an acceptable way. Girlish mannerisms for instance, can give others the impression that we are not to be taken seriously. Also, women often find themselves paralysed by the fact that faced with what they feel is unfair treatment at a meeting, they get a strong urge to cry. How can you be controlled, clear thinking and decisive if there are tears welling up in your eyes?

BULLYING AND CRITICISM

I had the unpleasant experience once, of watching a female director being bullied by her boss at a large meeting attended by all the senior people in the company. She stood up to him courageously at first, but as the bullying continued she was reduced to tears and her counter-arguments lost their effectiveness. It reminded me strongly of scenes I have witnessed of children at play. When little boys are bullied they usually stand up for themselves and persistently bash back. When little girls are on the receiving end of such treatment it is more usual for them to run crying to their mothers, who, of course, comfort them and may also chastise the bully. Unfortunately, this conditioning does little to help us to deal with grown-up bullies in public.

We often take things more personally than men, and when we receive unjustified criticism, bullying or unfair treatment in public tend to react very emotionally. When you are criticised in a meeting you have to make a choice about how you are going to handle it. If it's too much for you to deal with in public, then try just saying nothing in response, or using the fogging technique I described in Chapter 4 on assertiveness. It is often better to see your attacker in private after the meeting and tell him or her assertively that you did not think the remarks were fair or accurate. Whether the criticism is justified or not, it is wiser not to have a row in public; you will only make enemies.

If you are sufficiently in control of your emotions to deal with the criticism in public, then either quietly state your case, or apologise if you're in the wrong. Whatever you do, avoid getting defensive in front of everyone. Even if you are in the wrong, you can make a favourable impression by the way you handle yourself in such a difficult situation.

Phrases like these should be low-key enough to help you through the ordeal:

> Perhaps you're right, but I'm not sure. Let's talk about it in more detail after the meeting.

> Actually, John, I planned the project five weeks in advance, not one week. We had problems because of the postal strike, not because of inadequate planning.

> Yes, you are right. It was my mistake. I am sorry and I will give you my plans for putting it right tomorrow.

We also have to face the fact that most women in meetings where the majority of those present are male, say very little or nothing. Therefore, even if you do try to speak you may be ignored or interrupted because the others don't expect you, as a woman, to have anything to say.

Faced with these sorts of obstacles, how can we become influential at meetings? How can we overcome the numerous obstacles to our effectiveness and show to the world that we are worthy of being paid attention to? Much of the advice that follows would also be helpful to men. It demands skill and experience to be influential at a meeting and many men don't make the grade either. However, the problem is more common among women, so meetings skills are a significant weapon in the armoury of any woman who wants to be successful.

THE DANGERS OF SILENCE

It is dangerous to go to any meeting and not speak. Even though the other people there may seem to be getting on with their decision making and ignoring you, they will notice if you have nothing to say. The impression will be that you are either low-status, insignificant, ignorant or out of your depth. Even if some of these things are true, it is damaging to reinforce this impression through silence.

I know it can be very intimidating to be one of the few women at a large meeting, where everyone seems to be at home and to have a lot to contribute. Even after years of experience of that sort of event, I still have to make an effort to break into the male flow of words. Jean Denton says she has to force herself into the 'front row'. She needs to ask the second or third question, or else there is a danger that she won't speak. She finds that once she starts to speak she is less of a token woman in a world of senior men and more of a person with something to say.

Often, in the past, I have worked up the courage to speak, only to find that someone else started to speak at the same time. He was louder and more confident, and I lost my opportunity. I have learnt now not to let that happen – I just raise my voice and carry on, so that it's the other person who has to stop talking. It doesn't seem very polite, nor does it fit in with my conditioning to be supportive, but it is a survival tactic. Once I have spoken, clearly and constructively, it is easier to break in again. After my first intervention, I get the impression that people expect me to speak again, so I relax and feel more a part of the meeting and find it easier both to think clearly and to make relevant contributions.

So, even if you do think you are way out of your depth, spend the early part of the meeting searching for something to say and an opportunity to say it. A few short sharp points will boost your image and do more to gain you respect than hours of hard labour back in your office.

Interestingly, women who do speak at meetings receive a lot of favourable attention. Avril Hammil makes this point – people who go to meetings with her think she is on the ball and knows what she is talking about. It is not that she contributes anything clever, she says, it is because she speaks at all. People compare her favourably with women who don't speak at meetings, and this gives her a big advantage.

Once you overcome that hurdle and start to speak at meetings, it makes you feel very good. You get a glow of satisfaction from having got up the courage to do something difficult. It is also nice to get the attention and recognition which comes to those people who have had something positive to contribute. But what you say – and how you say it – is obviously important, too.

WHERE TO SIT

Where you sit at a meeting can have a lot to do with how easy or hard you find it is to join in the discussion. The best place is directly opposite the chairperson, and the second best place is in the middle of either of the side rows. In these positions most people can see you and you can easily signal that you want to speak. Research indicates that people in these positions do more talking than those sitting on the edges. Clearly, sitting where people can't see you is quite a disadvantage. As one of my interviewees remembers:

> Once, as a young manager, I had to attend a series of meetings with some very senior people in the company. I was very frustrated after the first meeting because I had found that no one listened to me and that it was hard to break into the discussion. At the second meeting I arrived early and sat opposite the chairman. This meeting went well for me and I had no difficulty in speaking when I wanted to. After that I always went for the same seat, and in the end the others would leave it free for me, even if I was late.

Improving your performance

Once you feel confident enough to speak at meetings, there are several things that you can do to improve your performance and make yourself more influential:

- *Voice* Most women (and many men) don't speak loudly enough at meetings. Meetings are a rat race, normally, with several people competing for a chance to be heard. Soft voices are too often ignored or not listened to. The appropriate volume is a little louder than the volume you would use in informal conversation, and a lot louder if you are softly spoken. Many people worry about their accents but I think the real issue is not the accent, but whether you speak clearly. Make a little extra effort to be heard and understood in a meeting, and particularly so if you are a woman.

  Nerves and tension often make us speak too quickly and scramble our words. Combine that with a soft voice and a tendency to mumble and it is not surprising that people choose not to listen. You need to find a pace that keeps the audience listening. The other disadvantage in speaking too fast is that it may make other people think either that you are nervous, or that you are trying to dominate them. Speaking too slowly is equally disastrous, as people get bored and stop listening. So listen to yourself when you speak, and deliberately slow down or speed up as necessary.

- *Eyes* Use your eyes in a meeting. They are an easy and effective way of getting people to pay attention to you. When speaking it is important to look around at the others, rather than down at your notes or out of the window. Equally important is the need to look at other people when *they* are speaking. This shows that you are alert and interested, and it is experienced by the speaker as being supportive. This encourages the speaker to address his remarks to you, and makes it easier for you to chip in after he has finished, if you want to. Many people spend much of the meeting with their eyes down. This signals boredom or deference and is not the message you want other people to take away about you.

- *Body Language* Your posture, facial expression and gestures give a lot of information to others about the way you are feeling, and this is particularly significant in meetings. They can be boring and frustrating and if you don't think about the way you look, it is very easy to slouch and scowl. Even in a busy meeting people will notice if your body language is signalling negative feelings. You need to look alert and interested throughout if you want to give a favourable impression. Sit up straight, but not rigidly – either lean slightly back, or forward on the table. Some leaning forward shows enthusiasm, but to do so the whole time shows a desire to dominate.

Managing the impression you create through thinking about these things – voice, pace, eyes and posture – is not difficult, it's just a matter of remembering to do it. It is possible to get carried away with the heat of an argument or the frustration of failing to get what you want out of the meeting, and to forget to think about your body language. Just remember it whenever you can, and over the years it will become a habit.

- *Dress* Many of the women I interviewed consider it vital to dress smartly when going to meetings. They feel that anything they can do to increase their status can only help. You will certainly be seen as less influential if you turn up for meetings in crushed clothes and scuffed shoes or, indeed, with un-combed hair. Remember, even in the most informal of meet-ings you will be competing with others for attention; if you dress well it may give you a head start.

KEEP IT SIMPLE

Most people's contributions at meetings are not succinct enough. Because these occasions are so competitive, it is very tempting, once you have got the floor, to say everything. This is a mistake because after a very short time people will stop listening and start planning what they are going to say in answer to your first points. If you have a lot to say, then break it up: make the first point, say you have some other ideas but that you want to discuss the first one before carrying on.

One good way of keeping your speeches brief yet interesting is to use simple words and sentence constructions. A few sharp, lucid phrases make much more impact than long convo-luted sentences. It helps to do some preparation before the meeting and know what you are talking about.

Consider the difference between these two interventions, which are both saying the same thing.

I consider it imperative that we terminate our contract with these particular suppliers because of the deterioration in their ability to respond to many of our demands, especially in the very important area of quality.

XY suppliers are reducing their quality. I propose that we stop using them.

There are many ways of being long-winded and boring in meetings. One way is to use long, formal words where short, simple ones would do. Here are a few examples:

Commence rather than Start
Transmit rather than Send
Positioned rather than Put
Accommodation rather than House (or Office)
Inform rather than Tell

Always go for the simple, familiar words. Your meaning will be clearer, your speech less formal and your contributions more interesting. People who are too formal in meetings are not just boring, they're pompous, and this is the last thing you want to be. Instead of saying something like:

I think we should commence the programme to acquire accommodation for these people. Please inform them that a delay of only a few months is anticipated.

Say this instead:

We need to start to find housing for these people. I suggest we tell them they'll only have to wait a few months.

You'll sound more human and be a lot easier to follow.

Another way of being long-winded is to use clichés, and unnecessary words and phrases which add nothing to your meaning. Indeed they obscure it. Here are some examples of unnecessary phrases:

At this moment in time
For your information
It is a matter of prime importance
From the viewpoint of

As far as meaningless words are concerned, fashions change with time. In the early 1970s the 'in' word was 'situation'. We had the meeting situation, the interview situation and I began to wonder when we would get the situation situation. It finally became so overused that I decided to drop that word from my vocabulary, even when it would have been appropriate to use it! Later in the 1970s the 'scenario' crept in. Soon it was on everyone's lips and the meeting situation was replaced by the meeting scenario. As the 1980s began I noticed that the fashion had swung over to 'unbelievable'. I went to few meetings where I did not hear this word. The 'in' word in the late 1980s is 'deliverables'. I'm not even sure if I know what it means.

I do understand the pressure to fill our utterances with these trivial words and phrases. Often we are buying time to think, and what is more easy than to do so with familiar padding words and clichés that spring to mind because we hear them so often. But it is far better to pause when we need to think, rather than to confuse the listener and lower the impact of what we have to say with these clichés. They are habit forming. Listen out for them when you speak and make an effort to avoid them.

Short, simple words and sentences make your meaning very clear; sometimes we hide behind padding, and long-winded phraseology because we haven't quite got the confidence to say what we think. This is where preparation before a meeting can be such a help. If you decide beforehand just what it is you want to say, and find an acceptable way of saying it, then you can be more direct in the meeting.

Another way of keeping your contributions brief is to make sure that everything you say is relevant and to the point. If you concentrate, and are clear about what is on the agenda and what the meeting is trying to achieve, then it is possible to keep your speeches to the point. You will certainly stand out and be impressive if you do this, because so many people in meetings irritate others by constantly wandering off at a tangent.

OTHER PREPARATION FOR MEETINGS
Doing other sorts of preparation before you go to a meeting often pays dividends. You can chat to people before the meeting in an attempt to drum up support for the things you feel strongly about. If the support is not forthcoming then at least you'll know why

before the meeting and may be able to adjust your case to take people's objections into account. If you meet objections for the first time in the meeting you may find it hard to think quickly on your feet and counter them effectively.

If there are items you want on the agenda, ask the chair if she (or he) will consider adding them on beforehand. Then you can prepare for them. If you haven't got access to the chair then ask someone who has if they will plead your case.

Gather all the informaton you need to get your proposals accepted. It is no good suggesting a new project or direction if you haven't done the costings, both for your proposal and the alternatives. Try to anticipate the questions and go prepared with all the facts and figures you are likely to need to be persuasive. If you have a lot of detail to impart, give some thought as to how you are going to present it. Visual displays can do wonders to make you look professional, as long as they are done well. Flip charts and overhead projectors are often available, do use them if you can.

Pre-meeting preparation will do a lot to make you look like the competent, credible person you are. It's so easy to give the wrong impression if, through lack of it, you can't get your act together in front of an audience!

POSITIVE REMARKS
Try to make positive rather than negative remarks. Usually you have a choice. For example, you could say either,

> For such an important meeting I think we should choose a time of day when we are all fresh and alert,

Or

> I think it is terrible that we have such an important meeting at a time of the day when no one is fresh and alert

People will be much more inclined to consider your proposals if they are put in a positive way. You will enhance your reputation if you are seen as someone who tried to seek solutions, rather than as someone who complains and puts other people down for the decisions they have made.

Aggression and negative remarks do more to damage a

woman's image than a man's; it is all too easy to get labelled as a whining, complaining woman. Being positive, even when you need to disagree with or modify a proposal, is the way to avoid this sort of label. If, for example, someone proposes that the way to increase sales of a product is to advertise on television and you disagree, you could deal with it in a number of ways. You could say:

I disagree. I think that television advertising is too expensive and it wouldn't be cost-productive. I really don't think that we should do that.

Or

Yes, but don't you think that you're going slightly over the top; television advertising is so expensive!

Or

Never! It's much too expensive. I think we ought to go in for point-of-sale promotion.

Each of these ways of expressing your disagreement is negative, and will be a put-down for the person who made the suggestion, even if you say it with a smile. (And when we are disagreeing with someone at a meeting we rarely smile, thus increasing the negative impact of our disagreement.) A more supportive and constructive way of dealing with this would be to say something like:

Television advertising is one option we should consider. I think point-of-sale promotion is another. In fact it may be more cost-effective. Why don't we list all the possible alternatives, consider their pros and cons, and choose the method that gives us the biggest increase in sales for the lowest cost.

By expressing yourself in this way you have avoided making an enemy by giving someone a put-down, and you are helping the meeting to be objective about making its decision. You have also avoided falling into another trap. Many traditional or insecure men are not accustomed to being disagreed with, and take it as a threat to their authority. When a disagreement comes loud and strong from a woman it can be quite difficult for them to deal with. In fact you may not have meant to challenge their authority; probably you were just expressing a different point of view. There is nothing to gain from inadvertently making enemies of people like this. Make all your contributions, even your disagreements, constructively and positively and you will make allies rather than enemies.

FLUENCY

Finally, try to speak fluently. Hesitations and speech errors are a big turn-off. Because of the competitiveness at meetings, people won't listen patiently while you painfully search for the right words through a forest of 'ums' and 'ers', and repeated phrases. This is the most difficult piece of advice to follow because, when you are thinking on your feet, it is very normal to be hesitant. The only remedy is to prepare as much as possible beforehand, decide what you want to say about the points that are on the agenda. Then at least you will only be hesitant when you are dealing with matters arising that you did not anticipate. If you habitually plan what you want to say beforehand, you will improve. Making some of your contributions well will give you the confidence to think clearly and this will help with those that are unplanned.

Being influential at meetings is not only about speaking well and looking alert, although that goes a long way. We also have to give some thought to what we speak about. Some people direct their remarks only to the subject that the meeting is about. If their speeches are clear and constructive, they will be seen as positive contributors to the meeting. However, another way of being constructive in a meeting is to make contributions which help the meeting to achieve its purpose: to make a good decision or to solve a problem. So, in a meeting which is deciding on a new training policy, you can either make proposals or supply information about training policy which is the subject of the meeting, or you can say things which help the others to come to a decision. Or, of course, you can do both.

What sorts of contributions can you make which will help the meeting to come to a decision? You can clarify points by asking questions or checking other people's assumptions. You can summarise from time to time so that people know what has been agreed so far. You can bring people into the discussion by asking what they think about a point. You can move the meeting forward by saying, 'So we all agree on that point. Let's move on to the next.' You can bring the meeting back to the point when people start to stray, be supportive by agreeing with what you consider to be sound or creative points, and add to these, thus developing them. For example, if a colleague says, 'I think our training policy should include induction courses for newcomers,' you can say, 'Yes, that's a good idea, and I think they should be two-day courses.' With this contribution you have both supported your colleague and developed his idea.

These sorts of contributions, which help the meeting to work better and come to a decision, need to be made, or else the meeting may get nowhere. The chair may or may not be doing these things. Any person in the meeting who contributes in this way is seen as being constructive. Supporting other people and developing their ideas is a good way of building allies. So many people inadvertently make enemies in meetings by disagreeing tactlessly, interrupting, being inattentive and giving negative messages with their body language. Asking questions and bringing other people into the discussion will help to build allies and make you seem less domineering in a meeting where you have a lot to say about the subject. Ally building is important because it is much easier to influence people who see you as supportive and receptive to their ideas. If you make enemies, then your suggestions will be resisted, even if they are sound.

It makes a big difference if you go to a meeting knowing what you want to achieve. Then you will be clear about which proposals to support and about the general direction in which you want to influence the meeting.

If you find yourself at a meeting and the topic turns to something you know little about, you may find it difficult to speak, simply because you don't know what to say. In these circumstances, try to make contributions of the sort we have been talking about, which help the meeting to work better and come to a decision. If one of the items on the agenda was nuclear physics you might have nothing to contribute on the subject matter, but do not remain silent. Ask questions, ask other people what they think, and summarise, or ask someone else to. You could also check progress and move the meeting on after each decision. You need not speak a lot, but do have something constructive to say from time to time.

THE ART OF CHAIRING A MEETING

Of course, if all meetings were expertly and sensitively chaired, then it would not be so difficult to make a positive contribution and a favourable impression. But life isn't like that. Not only are there a lot of inexpert and untrained chairpeople around, but there is a traditional male way of chairing a meeting (mostly the person in the chair is a man) which creates an atmosphere that can be frustrating and difficult for a woman. One woman commented that she found she had to learn how to cope with traditional male chairmen. She feels they don't bring out the best in people, nor do they encourage enough intellectual searching. There is a male club atmosphere with people giving typically male signals that you can only take things so far.

> In traditional organisations where all or most of the senior people are men they learn very quickly the balance between keeping in with the boss, and having something to say for themselves. They soon learn the pecking order – it's really about establishing territories. The chairman uses various signals like his body movement, eye movement, tone of voice and the way things are phrased to indicate whether a topic is open to discussion or whether it's gone far enough. When everyone is entrenched in this tradition, people tend to know what they dare to say and when to back off. They operate a sort of self-censorship, using the chairman's signals as a silent guide.

> A male chairman usually signals his authority by sitting at the top of the table rather than along one of the sides. He normally only speaks to people within their roles and rarely relinquishes leadership to let the discussion flow. Often he will draw up the agenda himself, and may only give a little time for items suggested by other people. Not *all* men run meetings like this, but it is common in more traditional sectors like manufacturing.

> I have been to meetings run by women which have been very refreshing in contrast. They do more co-ordinating than chairing and are not so concerned with establishing their authority and

128

status, and maintaining the pecking order. They let leadership move around the room according to the topic being discussed. They shape the meeting but let others lead on specific topics. They use the people at the meeting to explore issues in a freer way and encourage them to give their ideas and experiences regardless of their roles.

They are sensitive towards the people present and to how and when they want to contribute. This leads to a freer atmosphere intellectually and a more thorough investigation of each issue.

When a woman is in the chair herself, she can have more control over the atmosphere in the meeting. This interviewee says that she rejects the traditional male way of chairing. She prefers to be incisive about what the meeting is tackling, and encourages people to have a full role. However, even in a well-run meeting where everyone is encouraged to speak, you need to look enthusiastic and speak well in order to be influential.

DEALING WITH SEXISM IN A MEETING
What should you do if you're the only woman present and you're asked to pour the tea, or take the minutes? Don't make a fuss but don't do it. You can't maintain your image of an influential executive if you fall in with people's traditional stereotypes of women. Chances are there will be several men in the room who don't think that you should be treated like this, and they won't be impressed if you acquiesce. Smile, make a joke of it, but also make it clear that you won't do it.

The teapot is closer to you, Robert, why not try your hand?

No thanks, there are a lot of points I want to discuss. Taking minutes would be distracting.

That's not a good idea, nobody can read my writing. I'd prefer not to do it.

Any remark like this that deals with the request lightly but firmly should do. If they persist, don't give in. Try using broken record (see page 58), but keep smiling.

WHAT TO DO AFTER THE MEETING
When the meeting is over, make sure you remember to take whatever action you agreed to in the meeting. If you need to do something by a certain date, put it in your diary. You will feel (and look) a fool if at the next meeting you have to confess that you haven't done what you promised. Make a note of what other people have agreed to do, too. If it is in your interest that they take this action, then find a way of reminding them. A lot of action is agreed at meetings which never happens.

SUMMARY
To summarise, as a woman you have certain disadvantages at meetings and have to do a number of things to overcome them. People will not pay attention to you unless you make them. Look alert and interested throughout, and try hard to find an opportunity to enter the discussion. You need to make speeches that are short, simple, relevant and fluent, and you can only do this if you are well prepared. Speak loudly and clearly enough so that people listen to you. Most of all, be positive when you speak, and do all you can by being supportive and constructive to win allies rather than make enemies. It is worth putting time and thought into preparing yourself for meetings because they are occasions where people will be watching you and judging you.

Impressive performance on such occasions will be even more help to you in your career than the effort you put into the work you do back in the office.

8

Life and career planning

UNLESS A WOMAN PLANS HER WHOLE LIFE SHE MAY FIND THAT HER JOB PLANS RUN UP AGAINST LARGE OBSTACLES, eg.

WAA...WAA WAA WAA WA WAA WAA WA

It is essential that women should plan their lives and their careers. Men can get away with just career planning because they can often leave large chunks of their domestic lives to their wives. Even so, many of them could improve the quality of their whole lives if they followed the practical advice in this chapter. If a woman does not plan her whole life, including her working life, she may find that her job plans constantly run up against large obstacles.

Unfortunately, the difficulty of undertaking such a mammoth planning task puts many of us off doing any career planning at all. We are also strongly conditioned to keep our options open so that we can fit in with the needs of our husband and family. We are still slowly moving out of an age where the husband is the main breadwinner, and women are brought up to be the back-up service. None of this encourages us to take our career planning very seriously.

Even women who aren't married and live on their own tend to do little career planning because the same social conditioning works to discourage us from throwing ourselves wholeheartedly into planning our working lives.

Planning and goal setting are tremendously important in shaping your working life and opening up opportunities. Add to that planning for your life as a whole and you have a powerful motivational force.

TAKING CHARGE

There are other reasons, too, why most women do not do any career planning, and why we are so reluctant to take charge of our lives. The fact that women often, though not always, earn less than their husbands means they need to be the ones who are flexible. The knowledge that most of us will have children at some stage is another reason for adaptability. The big problem is that our traditional roles load our lives with uncertainty:

- Will or will I not get married or settle into a long-term relationship?
- Will my husband be transferred to Birmingham and, if so, will I have to give up my job?
- Will I want to stay at home and be a full-time mother when I have my babies?
- Will my baby-sitting arrangements work out?

The temptation in the face of this uncertainty is to take life as it comes, to react to problems as they arise, rather than to take charge of our lives and to plan things to happen the way we want them to. Add to this the fact that we are not conditioned to think long term and to plan our careers in the way that men are, and it is not difficult to understand why women are inclined to drift.

Colette Dowling's book *The Cinderella Complex* mentions other reasons why we tend to hold back from career planning. Overprotected, as we often are, by our parents, and raised primarily to be someone's left rib, we tend to feel deep down inside that it is not a woman's role to take responsibility for planning and achieving a worthwhile career which can support the family. With this subtle conditioning at work, bright, energetic young women may make a good start at their careers, but they rarely do so in a planned way. They keep their options open (often without realising that they are doing so) and wait for the arrival of Prince Charming who will care for them happily ever after. But Prince Charming, even if he does arrive, will not always look after us forever. The number of married women who *have* to work and the number of divorcees, single parents and young widows is proof of that. Yet even in the face of harsh reality, these expectations continue to colour our judgement and cloud our decision making.

It is a great insurance policy for a woman to achieve some degree of financial independence and not to rely too much on her husband's support. Being left or widowed can be very impoverishing, unless you have a good job and can protect yourself and your family against the worst effects of such a disaster. The other benefit of career growth and financial independence is that it does wonders for your self-esteem!

But you must do some forward-thinking if you are to achieve your personal and career goals. So many women are starry-eyed about the future when they are in their twenties, ten or twenty years later these same women have either withdrawn into child-rearing or are still at work but stuck in junior or middle grades. To overcome all the natural obstacles in your path you need to combine belief in yourself and ambition with some down-to-earth, detailed planning.

LOOKING FOR OPPORTUNITY

The point about setting goals and planning how to get there is that it makes you alert to opportunities. Grim determination to succeed is not enough. You need to know just what you want to succeed at, and what are the goals that mark progress on the way. So often we see people with moderate ability, marching steadily to the top of their field, while others with above-average ability never progress beyond the middle ranks. The difference is often that the achievers know what they want and plan how to get it. Because they have goals, they don't miss opportunities, and also know how to create openings for themselves.

It is easy to feel envious of these people, and to suspect them of being lucky. The thing about luck is that it happens to all of us from time to time, but it is the people who recognise and exploit their good fortune who really get the breaks. Looking back on my early career I can remember many occasions when opportunities came my way which I simply did not recognise as such! Once a senior person in the company I was working for arranged to meet me for lunch to discuss a project which he wanted us to collaborate on. Had I been on the ball I would have seen this as a chance to increase my visibility and win an important ally amongst the decision-making ranks. Instead I didn't see the importance of the occasion and even forgot to turn up for the lunch! Naturally our project did not go ahead.

THE NO-PLANNERS
Most of the women I interviewed did no planning in the early stages of their careers. They said things like,

> Career planning never featured in my life. I graduated with no clear idea of what to do.

> My life just evolved, I never made any plans.

> I am still keeping my options open. Marrying, or living together, changes your life and status.

> I didn't plan, I just studied the subjects I enjoyed.

Also, with a few exceptions, they had very poor information on career opportunities. We still have to face the problem that many career advisers have fairly limited ideas about what sort of employment is suitable for women. One woman said that she chose an actuarial career at college because it sounded more glamorous than teaching or accountancy. She feels that she made big decisions on very poor thought processes, and had no guidance to do otherwise. Some of the interviewees had help from professional parents in choosing their careers, but most did not.

THE PLANNERS
Three of the interviewees, Jennifer Rosenberg, Jennifer Haigh and Carey Labovitch, did plan their careers right from the start. Jennifer Rosenberg says,

> I knew even when I was a schoolgirl that I wanted an exciting career, rather than one that was dull and boring, I wanted to fulfil myself. I knew I wouldn't have a job that needed a university degree because I hated studying. On the other hand I had an entrepreneurial flair, even as a child. I did a lot of organising at school. At the bazaars and fairs my stalls made a lot more money than the others. I sold bunting for the coronation. I loved acting too, and used to put on shows at home, for which I also charged.

My first career choice was the theatre. I had drama training and even though I didn't pursue this it gave me poise and confidence which I have used to my advantage in other jobs. Because of my love of clothes I wanted to become a buyer. I applied for any job at Marks and Spencer because I hoped that I could find a way to become a buyer with them. I was very clear, right from the start about what sort of career I wanted. I was offered a job in the post room and took it, but used it as a chance to get noticed and to open up job opportunities.

I eventually did achieve my ambition and became a buyer for the store (see also Chapter 1), but then realised that what I really wanted to do was to run my own business. When the opportunity came to set up J & J Fashions, my own company supplying garments to Marks and Spencer I took it. The company has grown considerably since the early days. In 1987 we took over another company and increased our turnover by £10 million.

Looking to the future, I know I want to make J & J Fashions a bigger business but I want to stay in control. My husband and I own the company between us fifty-fifty. I don't want anyone telling us how to run the business. I will take advice, certainly, but I want to be in a position to make the decisions.

Jennifer Rosenberg was Businesswoman of the Year in 1987. Jennifer Haigh was equally impressive.

I began to use the Careers Advice Centre for job information when I was in my second year at university. So I knew which organisations I wanted to apply for. I also knew that to get into a top management position I would need experience in a number of different functions, and took jobs that progressively gave me that experience.

I finally achieved my aim: I became Personnel Director for Trebor Limited which is a company with 3,700 employees.

I never consciously made a choice between being wife, mother or careerist. Yet when I was in my twenties I worked very hard and put work before everything. When I got into my thirties I realised that this wasn't enough, that I wanted more balance in my life. More time for having fun with the people in my life, more holidays, more sleep when I want it, more opportunity to be physically toned up, more time to *give* to other people, and more time to enjoy my home.

Work is still pressurised but I do feel I have a more balanced life now. I wouldn't want to swap my life style with my male colleagues at board level. I feel I am more flexible and varied. Now that I am more senior I feel able to be more myself at work. I want to contribute as many of my personal qualities as possible to my job. I do think that for a senior woman it is possible to work and live differently from senior men.

I have always been willing to try things. I have taken the initiative about getting experience in a range of different types of jobs. I had to learn the content of each new job, but I found I could transfer the general skills. I think I got where I did because of four things. I worked hard (at first I felt that as a woman I had to be better than men, although I don't feel that any more). I am good at analysing things. I am very straight, there is no false image or sham about my achievements. I planned my career.

Jennifer Haigh was one of the nominees for Businesswoman of the Year in 1987. Since our original interview she has moved out of manufacturing into the service sector, and works for a smaller, more dynamic organisation. She is now Director of Personnel and Administration for British Satellite Broadcasting Ltd and continues to plan ahead for the future. As well as maintaining a balance in her life she wants eventually to either run an organisation or develop her own business.

Carey Labovitch has always been ambitious and artistic.

I was a student at Oxford in 1980 doing modern languages when I started *Blitz* as a university magazine. I spotted a gap in the market which was a life style magazine for men and women. I had a lot of luck, but I also took a lot of risks. If I hadn't taken them I would never have developed the magazine, which won the Guardian Best Graphic Award after the third edition. I then managed to get it distributed on a national basis. One of the people who contributed to the magazine became a partner to do the editorial work, while I always remained in charge of finances.

1984 was a turning point. *Blitz* was sold all over the world and I launched another two magazines. At twenty-seven I was the only magazine publisher who was female. I had to develop a good business sense, which I didn't know I had. I achieved things by simply being very stubborn. The business continues to grow and I see the new publications as my babies!

It was lucky that I started the magazine at university because I never thought of myself as a woman (and all the disadvantages that can imply) until I hit the outside world. Publishing is a very male world and the chairmen of other publishing companies like to wine and dine me to see if I am real!

Sometimes people try to rip me off because they assume that as a woman I must be naïve. People also often assume that I am a secretary. Sometimes I am amused.

I don't think that it is surprising that I can run a business. Women get intuitive sense of how to run a business, from running their households. I am not married now, but I don't see why I can't marry, have a family, *and* continue to run a business.

I try to be myself as much as possible, but of course I can't always be. For example, I had no time for a social life at all when I was launching the magazine. I have sacrificed some of my youth to *Blitz*.

Carey wants to build up a publishing empire. She had goals and a vision right from the start of her career and her achievements are impressive. I first interviewed her in 1987. When I spoke to her a year later she had made great strides. She had formed Cadogan Press Group, which is a holding company for all her other magazine companies. The business has expanded considerably, and now does contract publishing for other concerns, and merchandises products such as watches and lighters which sell through stores like Harrods. The company has also produced the *Blitz Book of Photography*, and has just had a third exhibition at the Victoria and Albert museum. The operation now has a turnover half as big again as last year, and has moved into new, larger premises.

Carey was the youngest ever nominee for the Businesswoman of the Year in 1987.

These three women were clear about what they wanted to do when they were very young. Although most of the other interviewees were not so clear-sighted at the start of their careers, they did learn the importance of career planning later on. June Campbell says,

I look at my career more clinically now. I want to get promoted and I know what to do to make it more likely. I am aware of the opportunities both without and within.

Angela Moxam feels that she still tends not to do much long-term planning but she is very good at spotting opportunities.

Avril Hammil did not do any career planning at the start of her career, but she began to do so later on.

There was never any planning for the future in our school curriculum. I worked out that I wanted to do science, but not to teach it. When I was graduating from university the careers advice I got was useless. My parents were working-class so they didn't pressurise me like middle-class parents would have. My father thought that success was all about charisma and luck. My mother applied a little pressure because she thought that if you got good exam results and found yourself unhappily married then you could leave because you could support yourself. But I never received any direction over my career.

Even now I keep going off on tangents to do what I enjoy rather than to further my career. I have been lucky though, because I have a large network of friends and business contacts. I use this network to get good new jobs.

I now know that I would like, eventually, to be a company chairman. I am therefore beginning to plan my career more. I already have experience in marketing, research and development, and sales. Next I have to work in finance. I don't have a clear goal in terms of the type of company I want to work for, but I do know that I want to progress to chairman. I also want to go somewhere with a decent climate! I am trying to become clear about what sort of person I am, because this affects the sort of job I go for. I can't be one sort of person at home and another one at work.

I have got on well so far because I am happy to take responsibility. People don't usually like taking decisions so when I come in and say, 'Here is what I am going to do, here are the details and the costs,' I usually get my way. I have learnt to say 'I'll do that then', rather than 'Can I do it?', or 'Do you mind?' I am also prepared to take risks because I am at a marketable age.

When I interviewed her, Avril was working for British Telecom in marketing planning on the new business development team. Since then she has moved to manufacturers Hanover Securities where she works in Eurobond Sales. So she is getting her sales experience in the financial sector.

Judy Presnell also started her career without any planning. She did get a degree and professional qualifications, but chose to study subjects she enjoyed, without any clear goals in mind.

However Judy now has a management job at Prudential Assurance and is in charge of three departments and eighty staff. She got there because she is ambitious and began to plan her career.

I found that as a woman in an organisation where most managers are men I had to *tell* people what my career expectations were. I don't want people to see me as pushy but I've got to make it clear that I want to move up. Otherwise they would assume that as I am a woman I am content to stay where I am.

I have always worked for the Prudential. I started out doing actuarial work. I was competent at that, but nothing more. I found when I was promoted to become department manager that I was really good at management so that's what I want to stick with.

When I first interviewed Judy she was a department manager. She wanted to be promoted within a year and sure enough she was. For the future she wants to move around within the company for job interest and to continue to move upwards in management. When asked if she wants to get to the top she said:

Life at the top is probably thrilling. A huge bit of me wants to be best and to be at the top. However, when I am being realistic, I know that there is more to life for me than work. I am prepared to work hard but not necessarily the constant long hours that life at the top demands. This could hold me back from getting to dizzy heights but I do want to keep on moving upwards.

These women have all learnt that in order to get on they need to think about where they want to go, and plan how to get there. But they also had to think about the implications for their lives as a whole. Some have chosen not to have children, others have to consider at what stage in their lives to have their children.

Jacky Woodhouse, who is also a manager at Prudential Assurance, had to think hard about this latter consideration. Although she planned to go back to work after a short break she realised that she would have to spend at least a few months away from work with each baby. She had to be established enough so that she could afford a nanny, but in a job where a short absence wouldn't be the end of the world. She had her children in her middle thirties when she was in her first big management job. Had she waited she may never have had children (or may not have been able to go back to her job). As she became more senior in the company an absence of three to six months would have been much too disruptive.

Fiona Price's career planning is all about building up enough capital so that she can have a choice. She wants her financial advisory company to be big enough by the time she is thirty so that she can start to achieve some of her important personal goals. These include getting married, having a family and living in the country. To give her the time she needs for these things she wants to change her profession to training and she has already begun to work as a trainer to prepare herself for this transition. To free her to do this she will need to have a company that is big enough to sell, or to employ another person with her skills to run it on a day-to-day basis.

Fiona spends a lot of time thinking about her career and her goals. She is typical of a trend among young women who establish themselves by working hard in their twenties, and then want to have a full personal life (including children) in their thirties, but also want to have a rewarding and demanding job.

PROMOTION

It is possible for a woman with a lot of talent, energy and luck to fall into a good job and to have a sparkling career, but this does not happen to many of us. Mostly what happens is that women who don't take charge of their careers and set goals get stuck at middle levels. Let me relate a typical story. Two bright young people join a company at the same time: one is a man and one a woman. They both apply themselves well to their jobs but the man does something extra. After being there a year he tells his boss that he is interested in a promotion and asks what the opportunities are. His boss sees that he is ambitious and since he has performed well is glad to help him to progress. The woman works just as well but says nothing to her boss about her aspirations. The boss assumes that, like most women, she is not ambitious. The woman notices that her male colleague gets promoted but that she doesn't, so she works even harder hoping that she will get noticed. Eventually she does the job so well, that her boss is completely dependent on her and would be loth to let her go even if he discovered that she had ambitions. But he doesn't make this discovery because the woman does nothing to make her aspirations known. The boss continues to employ her, but marvels that women are content to work hard at jobs that only use a fraction of their abilities.

There is another trap which women fall into that stops them from getting on as well as they could. I was first alerted to this problem by a sympathetic male manager who wanted to help his women staff to progress.

> I have a lot of trouble getting through to some of my female staff, some of them have great potential, and it's in my interest as well as theirs that they stay with the company and get promoted. They are very ambitious, but they don't see that it's up to them to do the planning and to learn the influence skills that would help them to get on. They tend to feel that since they work hard it's up to the company to reward them by giving them promotions. They feel bitter when they don't get these promotions and don't understand that it's up to them to set goals and go for them by learning the skills needed at higher levels.

Women do not need to remain stuck at junior and middle grades in undemanding jobs. We have the talent, energy and education for senior positions but we must plan our lives and careers to achieve them. I will now take you through a process that will help you to decide where you want to go and how to get there, but first you may need to confront one serious obstacle. This is the uncertainty factor. How can I plan my life and career, you may ask, when I have to keep my options open for marriage, babies, husband's or boyfriend's transfers etc? What I say to that is that plans can be changed. If you have clear goals, you can often find the best way to still achieve those goals when your circumstances change. All successful people have to change their plans at times, but this doesn't stop them from making them in the first place.

Getting into a senior position in your field may not be your career ambition. Women are not as programmed as so many men are to go for it or bust. We don't accept, necessarily, that other people's career ambitions should be our own. Jean Denton feels that the reason why more women aren't MPs is partly because they are too sensible to make such sacrifices to their personal lives. Although this can hold us back in some ways, it can also clear the fog and help us to make better decisions about what we want out of life.

So don't be put off this chapter if you feel you are not one of those people who wants a job at the top. Many of us have aspirations for our lives which don't include that sort of pressurised existence. The advice in this chapter *is* relevant for you even so, and it is no disgrace not to want to make it to the peak. If what you want out of life is simply a stimulating and worthwhile job and a happy and full personal life, then you still have to plan for it. Identifying what you want out of life, and then systematically planning how to achieve it is necessary for everybody. It is the people who don't plan who drift around and find themselves doing things they don't enjoy.

EXERCISE

To start the planning process it is useful to decide what it is you want out of life. Picture yourself five years into the future. Think of how you would like to be then in some detail:

- Where are you living?
- What does your house/flat look like?
- What does it cost (in today's prices)?
- Who are you living with?
- What work are you doing?
- What do you earn?
- What are your achievements?

To help you to do this well, close your eyes and see yourself at home, and at work. Try to imagine what you are wearing, how senior you are and your relationship with the people around you.

When you have done this think of three words that express the sorts of things you are aiming for in your life and hope to achieve in the next five years. Write these words down.

When I first did this exercise the three words I chose were

power, elegance and fun. Within a year of doing this I had become director of my own company (power), I had redecorated the house and changed my life style slightly and my clothes (elegance), and I had created more time for the children and leisure (fun). I then repeated the exercise and found that my priorities had changed and I therefore changed some of my words and made a new set of plans.

Overleaf is a chart which you can use to make action plans for achieving what you want out of life. The chart encourages you to decide on specific activities to achieve your goals and target dates. When setting your goals use this as a guide to ensure that they are realistic and achievable.

CHECKLIST FOR EFFECTIVE GOAL SETTING

1   Make it *specific* rather than general. For example, to increase sales of x by 20 per cent within the next three months, rather than simply – and vaguely – to be better at selling.
2   Is it geared towards *action*? That is, what will I be *doing* in working towards my goal?
3   Is it *realistic*? Is it truly attainable or am I setting my aim too high? (Several) small goals are more attainable and therefore more likely to be successful.
4   To what extent am I fully *involved* with the goal? Or is its achievement dependent on a number of other people?

When you have completed the action planning chart you need to make sure that you actually do the things that you have planned. The best way of ensuring this is to find another person you trust, discuss your ideas with them and fix a date on which you are going to report to them that you have taken the steps on your action plan.

Action planning is not a magic formula for achieving career goals, but it does help you to make important decisions about your life. You may find when you are setting goals that there are some immovable obstacles either at work or in your personal life. Doing this exercise will help you to decide things like whether a change of job, or even career, is needed. It will also help you to make important personal decisions like:

ACTION PLANNING

GOAL What do I want to achieve	ACTIVITIES What will I be *doing* in working towards my goal?	HELPING FORCES What or who will help me reach my goal? (list)	HINDERING FORCES What or who will hinder me reaching my goal? (list)	HOW CAN I INCREASE THE HELPING FORCES? (list)	HOW CAN I REDUCE THE HINDERING FORCES? (list)	TARGET DATE
						REALITY CHECK Is it all worth it?
						If not, review the original goal

144

- Can I accept a transfer to London without irreparably damaging my personal life?
- Do I want to have children or would I be happier devoting myself to my career?
- Is now a good time to have a career break for starting a family or should I wait another year?

Decisions of this importance cannot be taken lightly, and they need to be discussed with others. If you have a clear set of goals, and know what you want out of life, you will find it easier to find your way through the maze of choices that life can present you with.

When you do your life and career planning you may find that your goals are in conflict with those of the other people you live with. A friend of mine recently went home fired with enthusiasm after attending a seminar on career planning and goal setting. She did the exercise included in this chapter and showed the results to her husband. He decided to do it himself. They then got together and compared notes. What they found was that my friend wanted to up the ante, do more stimulating work and continue living in London where she could get that work. Her husband's goals were quite different. He wanted to live a more peaceful, less frenzied existence, and move his business and family to the country. They are now settling down to some lengthy negotiation and *both* realise that they may have to make compromises. At least they both know where they stand and what they have to do next.

I am a great believer in life and career planning. I didn't start to do it until my late thirties, by which time I had become stuck in a middle position in my profession. I was working as a freelance management trainer and not enjoying it all that much. I was getting lots of jobs but I was having to be away from home a lot, and working much too hard. It was very tiring and not much fun. Also I was not getting the opportunity to use my consultancy and organisational skills. As a result of attending a course for women managers, I began to plan my career. I decided to aim for

- More highly-paid work in the private sector.
- More short-course work (two-day courses) so that I wouldn't have to teach all week.

- More work in London so that I wouldn't have to be away from home all the time.
- More consultancy work.
- More projects where I was in charge so that I could use my organisational skills.

The results of planning were amazing. Even though I was not sure at the planning stage how to achieve some of my goals, what was important was that I became clear about what I wanted.

The first thing I did was to telephone all of my contacts in the private sector and tell them I was looking for work. I also asked my husband to try to get leads for me among his clients. I followed up all enquiries with great enthusiasm, even though it meant having meetings late in the evening after a day of teaching. I took the initiative to end a big contract which, although it made me feel financially secure, was keeping me too busy to look for new clients. This was a big risk but I felt it would pay off. It did. I was asked by BIM (British Institute of Management) to run a public course for them which we called 'The Influential Manager'. Again this was a risk because we could not be sure that the course was going to be popular. It was, however, and it led to a lot more work in the private sector.

Within nine months of making my first plans I had achieved all my goals. The goal-setting exercise had made me alert to opportunities and I grabbed them as they came along. Goal setting and planning has now become a habit and I have a review about twice a year. I often find that I want to change my priorities because my circumstances have changed, or because I have learnt more about myself.

One interesting outcome of my goal setting was the writing of this book. I had never written a book before and certainly did not see myself as a writer. I had, however, set a goal of getting more publicity in order to help my business to grow bigger so when the idea of writing this book was presented to me, I could see that it stood a good chance of helping me with this goal. Even my research for the book gave me some useful work contacts. Writing the book will also enable me to achieve some personal aims I have, to help women achieve their potential. Fearsome though the task seemed to someone who had no writing experience, I decided to go ahead.

Life and career planning should be a combination of fact and fantasy. The fantasy comes first where you use your imagination to visualise the sort of life you want to be leading. Let your imagination work for you here. Picture yourself in all the sorts of situations you would really like to be in. A good imagination is a powerful motivator.

Then come the facts. It's at this stage that you begin to look at reality and do the detailed planning that you need to ensure that your dreams come true. And don't forget to share your plans with your partner if you have one. Plans that have his support and backing are more likely to be achieved. If you find you haven't got his support, then at least you know what one of your obstacles is, and you can plan how to overcome it, or develop a compromise which achieves your highest priority goals.

Don't let the hurdles put you off from planning. You can overcome most difficulties if you keep your eyes open for opportunities to do so. The point is that only those of us with clear goals will recognise those opportunities when they arise.

9

Taking risks

Risk-taking is essential for getting on and getting to the top: 'Nothing ventured, nothing gained'. To take advantage of opportunities you often have to take risks because the outcome cannot be guaranteed. But you have to take opportunities when they come your way because they provide you with career openings.

People who get to the top may seem lucky to others, but often the truth is that they are courageous rather than just fortunate. They got the breaks because they took the risks. To get on in most organisations you need to get noticed, but doing good work is usually not enough. You have to find a way of putting yourself in the limelight. Again this carries a risk: you could make a fool of yourself in front of somebody important, or suffer a public failure, but in order to get on you must put yourself on show from time to time. You will learn, both from your successes and from your failures. You will also learn that failing is not the end of the world, and the next time you have to take a risk, it will seem a little less frightening.

TAKING OPPORTUNITIES

There are two main types of risk that we have to face at work:

- The major job risk is where you are faced with a career opportunity or decision, like the chance to work at a senior level in a new company or department, and you have no way of being absolutely sure if it is going to work out. Jennifer Haigh was offered a very promising job at a certain stage in her career and no one could guarantee that it would last for more than a year. She assessed the risk, realised that if she could make it work it would be a leap forward for her, and took the job. It did work out and she is now a board director. These sorts of risks are not everyday affairs, but they are presented at intervals in everyone's career.
- The second type of risk is less dramatic, but a much more frequent occurrence. There are numerous occasions in our day-to-day work when we are faced with challenges and opportunities which we find frightening. These may range from a chance to do a demanding high-profile project to a request to make a complicated presentation at short notice. Usually these day-to-day risk situations are about doing things which make us more visible. They present us with both the opportunity to become known and to make achievements publicly, and the danger of public failure if we don't get it right.

One of the significant factors that distinguishes successful people from others is that they are prepared to do things which contain an element of danger. This chapter examines how playing it safe can harm women's careers. It presents ways of challenging the conditioning that prevents us from taking risks, and gives guidelines on how to take calculated risks.

PLAYING IT SAFE
The natural reaction for many people, particularly women, when faced with risky situations is to play it safe, to avoid failures. Why should women in particular be so inclined to avoid risk-taking? I think the answer, once again, goes back to the way we are raised. In general, whereas boys are raised to perform, girls are raised for partnership. We are trained in the art of giving love and nur-turance, and in winning love from other people. While boys' competitive drives are encouraged, in girls they are ignored or dampened down. No one prepares us for the fact that to be a

success we must be competitive, and that part of the reality of competition is that we must face the risk of losing.

Women are actively discouraged by society from being competitive. Disturbing images of competitive women are presented in the comic strips. We begin to see competitiveness as the darker side of femininity, as ladies fighting with their handbags. We therefore grow up with no practical experience in the rules that make competition safe and we fear its ferocity. We don't learn how to lose, so as adults we keep this fear of failure, and prefer to play it safe rather than to take risks. Needing to be liked and loved, we fear that if we take risks and do better than our colleagues, then we will lose their friendship.

Boys, on the other hand, learn that if you beat your friend at football it will not kill him and he will not hate you forever – besides there will be another game tomorrow and maybe he will win then. Boys are taught that competition, taking risks and winning is natural, not a betrayal of one's friends and, in fact, it can even lead to deeper friendships. A young boy cannot get through adolescence without learning how to take defeat, and how to win without destroying his opponent. All of this leads him to feel easier about sticking his neck out and taking risks as an adult. Only girls lucky enough to excel at competitive sports grow up with these lessons learnt.

Not surprisingly, therefore, women are notoriously bad at taking risks. There have been the heroines who have flown the Atlantic single-handed and climbed Mount Everest, but, as a sex, we do tend to play it safe if we have a choice. We do not learn that it is all right to fail sometimes, and therefore how to learn from failures. We also do not experience the exhilarating sense of being a victor, and of fighting against the odds to become one.

On the other hand, women cheerfully face one of the biggest risks of all: that of being pregnant and giving birth. We go into childbirth often badly informed, with the fear of God put into us by many people, knowing that it is going to be painful. Yet with our eyes on the rewards at the other end we are courageous. I think we should take heart from this and see ourselves as beings designed to survive fear and pain.

The tendency to play it safe may be something natural

within us, built in to protect us and our children. We shouldn't only see it as something negative, because it also helps us to survive. Stress-induced diseases such as heart attacks and ulcers *are* more prevalent amongst men and we would be foolish to follow them down that particular path. I am not trying to make a case for women to become as macho, aggressive and competitive as all the real men who don't eat quiche! On the contrary, trying to base our behaviour on male models is as inappropriate in risk-taking as it is in power and leadership. We need to find a feminine way of coping with this problem, a way which values competitiveness and risk-taking as success behaviours, but that includes strategies for collaboration and survival.

Elisabeth Kershaw had this to say about her approach to risk-taking and competition.

> I love competition. Wouldn't life be dull without it! I think there is no point on working hard to come fourth or fifth – I want to work hard to win. But *my* way is to use my skills to get there. If you have to use back stabbing to keep your job or to get on, then you shouldn't be there.

Fiona Price has a similar point of view.

> I have to compete a lot, both in business and in sport. Some people approach competition by trying to put the other person down. This does produce results but it is not the way I prefer. I like to do well by improving my performance so my main competition is against myself. Can I do better than I did last time? Have I learnt enough from the last frightening thing I did to make it easier and better next time? I am in Finance, which is one of the most competitive sectors there is, yet I feel quite comfortable about being there. This is because I really feel I have something to offer, that I can create a niche and add something of value.

Back in the 1950s a psychologist called McClelland did some research into why some people were inclined to be achievers, and why others weren't. Two of the significant factors that he found in achievers were awareness of the rewards of success and reasonably high expectations of achieving them. Where these factors were present, people were more inclined to take risks and try. The factors present in low achievers were fear of failure and low expectancy of success. So many of us women have these background factors working against us:

- We are not tuned in to the rewards of success. On the contrary, we may be punished for success by our envious friends.

- Our fear of failure is often high, because we are not encouraged as children to compete and take risks. We do not learn that we can cope with failure.

- Only in those cases where the task seems easy because it's within our area of expertise do we have a high expectancy of success. In other cases, where the task seems difficult, we expect to fail because we haven't learnt to stretch ourselves. With our policy of playing it safe, we don't discover what we are capable of doing.

THE LITTLE-WOMAN SYNDROME
Another problem which can inhibit women from risk-taking is the traditional view of femininity. This view says that it is feminine and attractive to be weak and vulnerable and by being like this we will get a man to protect us. We grow up depending on our fathers for protection and then pass these dependency needs on to our husbands. Associated with this is the traditional view that the strong and brave and responsible in our society are the men. Men grow up with the realisation that they will have to earn for themselves and probably for their families too. Although most women have worked throughout history, we are still brought up to feel that it is desirable to marry. When we do that, we can rely on the steady income of our husbands, even if we earn as well.

AVOIDING RISKS
Recently I was on a boat when a sail got stuck and somebody had to climb the mast. There was a fierce wind and big seas and the boat was thrashing about. Everyone was nervous of going up the mast. There were three light people, two men and me. I was the lightest and would have been the easiest to pull up the mast, but I didn't even offer to go up. I just assumed that one of the men would do it. In fact they both offered to be pulled up, although

152

one admitted to being scared silly at the thought. The man who did climb the mast had a difficult and frightening time up there, but he did the job and when he came down he was the hero for the day. He certainly felt great for having done it. I envied him his achievement and wished I had not ducked out. The point is that I felt I *could* duck out because I was a woman, whereas the men knew that one of them had to do it, and both were prepared to take the risk and the responsibility.

Because we grow up with the feeling that we have the option to back away from risks, we don't learn how to cope with them. As a result, when each new risk comes up we feel frightened and the temptation to back away is strong. Anxiety is caused by uncertainty and fear of failure. The only way to lower this uncertainty is to face up to challenges and to discover that either we have the resources to do the task, that it's not as difficult as it appears, or that we can cope with a failure, and learn from it. If we don't take these risks, we continue to live with our fear of failure.

You don't need to remain stuck with anxiety and fear of failure. If you want to start facing up to challenges and grasping exciting opportunities you can learn how to take risks.

The first step is to try to become clear about how risky it is to play it safe. Avoiding challenges to avoid failure is a way of guaranteeing failure in the long run. It means a career of missed opportunities, low visibility and low growth. We cannot afford to take the risk of not taking risks!

LEARN TO ASSESS YOUR RISKS
'Take risks,' says Jean Denton, 'but don't take risks you can't afford to lose.'

One way of making it easier to take risks is to have a reliable method of ensuring that the risk you are taking is a calculated one, and not a dangerous gamble. Here are some guidelines to help you with risk taking:

Ask yourself these questions before making a decision.

- What do you stand to achieve by taking the risk?
- What will you learn, either from success or failure?
- What are the likely consequences of failing?
- What are the worst consequences of failing?
- Can you cope with these?

- What can you do beforehand to make success more likely?
- What are the possible alternatives?
- What would happen if you took no action, short term and long term?

This is how one young woman used this checklist to help her to assess a risk. She had been asked by her boss to take some action to increase the company's sales of training courses to the outside world. She proposed extra advertising and using a public relations expert, but these things were already being done. She then realised, with horror, that she was being asked to sell training courses by telephoning personnel directors out of the blue – 'cold calling' in other words. This felt like a high-risk activity to her because she was a trainer and had no selling skills and she feared she would make a mess of it. She assessed the risk by asking herself the questions on the checklist. These were her answers:

- *What do you stand to achieve by taking the risks?*
  I could increase the sales of training courses, contribute to the growth of the training department and would probably be earmarked for promotion.

- *What will you learn either from success or failure?*
  I will learn to cope with the unpleasant experience of people rejecting me over the telephone. I will learn how to talk to strangers and in a few words interest them in my proposition. I will learn how to do something that I find frightening!

- *What are the likely consequences of failing?*
  I will not contribute to the growth of the department. I won't get an early promotion. I will feel a personal sense of failure.

- *What are the worst consequences of failing?*
  I could be looked down on by my colleagues and my boss for not pulling my weight.

- *Can you cope with these?*
  I would hate it, but if I continue to do well as a trainer at least I won't be a total failure.

- *What can you do beforehand to make success more likely?*
  I could go on a selling course, and plan my sales patter very carefully.

- *What are the possible alternatives?*
  I could refuse to do it, claiming lack of skill and experience. I could offer to do it in the future after I had gained more experience with face-to-face selling. Neither of these alternatives meet the pressing need the department has to get more business *now*!

- *What would happen if I took no action?*
  If I didn't do the cold selling I would look very chicken-hearted to my boss and colleagues. They wouldn't force me to do it but they would be disappointed. I wouldn't learn whether I could make a success of it or not, so when I get an opportunity to sell in the future I will still feel anxious about it.
  I guess I'd better give it a try!

The trainer in the story did do the cold calling. Even though she went on a sales course and prepared herself well she found it very hard, she would sit at her desk with pages of names and phone numbers and try to think of something less unpleasant to do. She stuck with it though, in spite of some rather offensive rejections, and began to learn some important things. The first was the elation of getting a positive response. If someone said, 'Yes, I'm interested' it made all the other negative phone calls worthwhile. And she learnt that if she made enough calls the number of positive responses increased. She also learnt how to sound as if she knew what she was talking about, and as if she had a reasonable proposition. As she became more skilled, the unpleasant experiences reduced and the 'yesses' increased. In the end she became hardened to it and was able to 'cold call' whenever necessary.

As often as not, if you do a risk analysis, you will discover that the pay-off for your career and personal growth makes it worthwhile, and that you can live with a possible failure. If you can persuade yourself over a period of six months to take a whole series of risks, some small, some bigger, you will find that it leads to personal growth and an increase in self-confidence. People will notice.

Try not to tune into the natural tendency to say, 'No, I can't. It's too difficult, risky, uncertain.' We cannot stop ourselves having this reaction: all our upbringing leads us towards it, but we can become aware of what we are doing. This then gives us the choice of going along with it or not. Sometimes our instincts are right and we should obey them. In many cases, however, they are inappropriate and harmful.

Rethinking the decision to say, 'No, I can't' is a start, but it isn't easy. We have many subtle ways of backing out of things we don't want to do. Getting sick, double booking, missing the train are all ways of avoiding the issue. So we have to confront our decision-making processes at an early stage, before the automatic reaction takes over.

STRATEGIES FOR RISK-TAKING

Many of the women I interviewed for this book admitted that they were not natural risk-takers, but had all developed a strategy to help them to undertake frightening tasks. Angela Moxam is a good example. When she is frightened, her fear churns away inside her and can lead to nights without sleep. She forces herself to recognise it, confront it and then do something about it. Often, before she can act, she has to put her fear into perspective. She asks herself, 'What is the worst that could happen?' When she feels that she could cope with the worst, then she takes the risk. She now realises just how much she can learn from taking certain risks, and she does so more and more.

Some of the other interviewees had learnt to say, 'Yes, I'll do it' (against their natural instincts), and then to go and talk it over and get advice, guidance and support.

There are few situations that seem more frightening than having to play a tough tennis match, before a large, paying audience, and feeling you're under pressure to win. I think we can learn something about performing when we're frightened from Annabel Croft's experiences.

The power of positive thinking is far greater than anyone can imagine. I found when I got to be the number one that I was not just playing for myself, but for the sponsors, for the crowd and for England. When I was playing well I enjoyed it, but if I wasn't feeling confident it was awful. I had to learn how to block out the crowd and the negative thoughts when things were going badly. During these bad patches I learnt to change my tactics and try something different. You just can't get down on yourself. If you look depressed there is no way you can avoid feeling it, and it does affect your game. I often saw the effect of positive thinking on other tennis players. I could see these players physically change on the court as their minds changed. I could see how positive thinking made one player hit harder, and how this change in her made her opponent lose confidence and begin to hold back.

I also had to learn how not to feel terrible after I lost. My coach helped me to see a match as healthy competition, rather than as something terrible to lose. He showed me that fighting a good fight was what it was all about. It took me a long time to learn that, but it's an attitude that does help you to feel less nervous.

The things I learnt about facing the fear of failure help me a lot with my new job as a television presenter. I was very nervous the first time I stood in front of a camera, but I got better and better as I did more programmes.

This new job on 'Treasure Hunt' did feel risky to me because I am a tennis player, not a presenter. However, now that I've tried it I find I like it, and I am feeling confident about taking on something else in television.

Fiona Price has also had to face fear and risk in her business, but she has never failed to bite the bullet.

I have always been self-employed. I came into my financial business straight from college. I often suffered a feeling of nausea with the anxiety that my clients would know more than I did because I was so inexperienced. The only thing to do was to just have those awful feelings and do the job anyway. If you do face the music frequently enough you learn two things about your clients:

They often don't know as much as you and you *do* have something to offer.

If they are unpleasant to you it's usually because they've had a bad day, and it's not a personal rejection.

I have never failed to take an opportunity, however frightening it seemed. I don't want to live by regretting. I think I gain from all my experiences, good or bad. When something isn't going well I have learnt to acknowledge my negative emotions. You've got to go with these feelings. They are short-lived, and underneath a creative thought is probably bubbling which will help you to deal with the situation.

I am fundamentally optimistic. I know that I'm going to succeed on my terms, it's just a question of how, where and when. I feel it would be impossible to succeed without the experiences I am having now, the good and the bad, the successes and the failures. This is all part of the foundation.

Normally I just do what I do, even though it may be frightening, and I don't think about the risk. Once a thought came to me: 'Suppose you go bust next week – you could lose your house!' I just made the thought go away. You create what you picture mentally. If I imagine failure too often I would create it.'

Elisabeth Kershaw has similar feelings about the danger of contemplating failure.

I never think about failure. I am not going to fail! If you think you're going to fail, you never get started. You do things because you make a judgement that they are going to work. The risk is that you may make less money than you wanted to. I just think about how to get it right, not, 'What if I fail?' If you're satisfied that you've tried hard, then you don't feel bad about failure.

Linda Agran actually feels that it is very important to have failures:

I've learnt far more from my failures than any success I've ever had. Don't protect yourself (or your daughter) from possible bad experiences. Obviously you want to avoid fatal experiences like drug addiction and AIDS, but aside from these things we really need to live through disasters. How else can you learn how to cope with life? Women have got to find out what they want and who they are and they can only do this by experimenting and making mistakes.

The benefit of risk-taking is that it develops your judgement. You will soon learn which risks are worthwhile and which are not. Start with small things and build up your strength, confidence and judgement for the big issues in your life.

To summarise, it is dangerous to avoid taking risks, because it will retard your personal growth and reduce your career opportunities. To begin the process of risk-taking, confront your tendency to play it safe and learn how to take calculated risks and not gambles. Face up to your fear and accept it as part of the pain of developing. You will learn both from your successes and your failures, thus improving your strength and judgement. And remember, the biggest risk of all to your career is to avoid taking one.

10

Managing your domestic life

Most successful men have wives to look after them and if they happen to be bachelors or lose their wives, they are usually clever at getting someone else to sort out their domestic lives. Working women have no such advantage. Not only do they not have wives, but they are often someone else's wife (and mother) as well as having a busy job. Whereas women have the reputation of being good delegators at work, they don't seem able to transfer these skills into their home lives. 'Why not?' I asked Jean Denton who was the first interviewee to make this point. 'Because of their guilt,' she said.

We may feel guilty because we are playing a role other than the one which we were conditioned to play, and we are not devoting ourselves full-time to our 'primary' role. This guilt is the block to being effective about delegating domestic chores and responsibilities at home. Although working women do seem to have the energy and ability to handle a dual career, that is one which includes a domestic role, domestic responsibilities which are too heavy can be a real hindrance. If we overload ourselves with too much to do, too many conflicting interests and worries, we may find ourselves doing nothing really well, neither job nor home making.

TRYING TO BE A SUPERWOMAN

It is very difficult to get rid of all our domestic tasks and responsibilities and, indeed, we may not want to, especially those involving our children. In spite of the advantages of being less tied to domestic chores, many working women still exhaust themselves by trying to be superwomen and doing everything. In some cases there is little choice:

- Their income may be too low to afford paid help.
- They may be single parents with young children and therefore with no able-bodied adults or teenagers with whom they can share their tasks.
- They may have partners who travel so much or who work such long hours that they effectively become single parents.

On the other hand, there are an appreciable number of career women without such serious disadvantages. They either have the income for hired help, or they have adults or older children with whom they can share their chores. Yet in many cases these women do not let go, they do not delegate at home.

What is the price we pay for not delegating enough of our domestic responsibilities? Many senior jobs demand heavy commitment. If we are seen as having other major responsibilities it can affect promotion decisions against us. Sometimes we show our conflicting interests in subtle ways. Extra tiredness may take some of the enthusiasm out of our approach to work, or simply make us snappy or defensive. It may also make us disinclined to get involved in the after-work contact-building that can be so helpful to influence and progress. If we constantly decline invitations to dinners, meetings, conferences etc because they cut into the time for domestic chores or parenting, we cannot take advantage of the informal network which is so crucial to someone trying to build a career.

The result can be isolation. The decision (or necessity) to be a career woman cuts us off from the day-time social life of women who stay at home. Promotion to more senior jobs cuts us off from a lot of female company at work, because there are fewer women at senior levels. If we have to spend all of our leisure time doing household chores, then we cut ourselves off from informal contacts with other people at senior levels, either male or female. We can end up with few opportunities to make friends at work, and no one to care for us at home, since we are either living alone or doing all the looking after there.

LEARNING TO SHARE

The case for sharing domestic responsibilities with someone else is a strong one. It reduces tiredness and anxiety, gives us a chance to make more contacts and to perform at our best at work. It also gives us a feeling of support because someone else is helping. Most important of all, it gives us the opportunity to be more flexible and able to respond to unexpected crises or opportunities which encroach into our after-work time. This sharing can be done with partners, older children or paid home help. The point is that it is very important that we don't take it all on our own shoulders.

The conditioning which says to us that home and children are a woman's duty is very powerful. Very few of us can claim to be free of feelings of guilt if we try to offload some of these duties. There is a whole choir of little voices inside of our heads singing out messages like:

It's not right to ask someone else to clean up my own mess and dirt.

The domestic scene is my responsibility. If I hand it over to someone else I lose one of the few areas where I have any authority and control.

My standards for housework are high. Things must be done a certain way. No one can do things the way I do them.

If you want something done well, do it yourself.

The way I show love is to look after people. This means doing their cooking, cleaning and sewing.

Which of these tapes do you have playing in your head? Put a tick against those that seem familiar, and add any others you have. Our conditioning is so strong that either we feel guilty about going against these messages, or we obey them without question. When I interviewed career women for this book I found many examples of this process at work.

One senior woman suffered from guilt when she first considered hiring a cleaner. She felt it wasn't right to ask someone else to clean up after her. Her mother had not had a home help when she was a child, so she felt bad about hiring someone herself. In the end she decided that she needed someone to help her, and if it was OK with that person, then it would be all right with her. So she went ahead.

Having very high standards can also be a block to delegating chores to someone else. Another woman who is a single parent of two boys, an office administrator, and studying for a degree, mentioned that she hits patches of extreme tiredness and suffers from stress backaches. She genuinely has a lot on her plate, but she recognises that one of the ways of easing a busy patch would be to buy pre-cooked meals from the supermarket, and she cannot bring herself to do it.

> I like to buy and cook fresh meals because I know where it's been. I also like things done a certain way so cleaners annoy me if they don't do things as thoroughly as I would.

She realises that she is overloading herself by maintaining such high standards and refusing to delegate. However, to counter these feelings she has to sit down and think about them and try very hard to be rational. Interestingly, this person recently had an accident in which she hurt her foot and could hardly walk. The crisis forced her into delegating her household chores and depending on help from others, including her children. For example, she got her mother to buy pre-cooked meals, and her sons to put them in the oven! It worked, and saw her through her recuperation.

WANTING TO BE A 'REAL WOMAN'
Another block to being rational about delegating home chores is the conditioning that says we are not real women unless we are super housewives, whatever else we may be as well. If the house is in disorder it's the woman who feels guilty, while her husband is more likely to feel angry or indifferent. A man will not usually see

a dirty house as his responsibility, so he is unlikely to feel guilty. One of the women I interviewed felt when she first married, that she wanted to be the good little wife, and did all the cooking and ironing. She soon found it was too much for her and, to her credit, she negotiated with her husband for a fair system for sharing the housework.

Not all of us are able to handle these situations and make decisions about domestic chores with such calm rationality. One woman consultant puts it this way:

My house gets dirty and disorderly sometimes because I don't have a cleaner and things get on top of me. Of course I feel badly about it when the house is in chaos. Now my husband will come in, notice the mess and do something perfectly rational about it like start hoovering or suggest we get a cleaner. I immediately feel guilty and resentful, imagining that he is being critical of me for being such a slob. When I get cross with him for putting me down about housework standards he is really surprised, because he was simply being practical and meant no criticism at all.

In fact he likes me to work and doesn't think I ought to waste my time worrying about housework. So why do I take his remarks so personally? It's this awful conditioning that society lumbers us with, that the house is a woman's responsibility and when things aren't neat and clean we have failed in our womanly duties. I therefore imagine that everyone feels critical of me when the house is untidy, whether they do or not.

The same thing can happen over remarks made about my children by people who aren't career mothers like myself. If anyone criticises my child, or notices anything wrong with them, even something small like a tear in their clothes, I get upset inside. I get the sneaking feeling that they are implying that the child is less than perfect because I am an absentee mother and that makes me feel really defensive. Sometimes people are getting at me, but mostly they aren't. It's my own guilty feelings that get in the way of me taking those remarks at face value.

One of my interviewees, a powerful and successful woman who could afford a small army of housekeepers, comes home from work at about seven-thirty in the evening and spends from then until eleven-thirty cooking, washing up and sorting out the laundry.

When I have finished my chores I am exhausted. In fact I am tired a lot of the time, but I have got to do everything well, to be a perfectionist. It's not enough to be successful at work – I see myself also as the original frontier woman, wonderful mother and wife.

LETTING GO

Often a woman's only experience of power is to run her own household. When other people take over and do things differently it can be very unsettling.

When my children or my husband cook they make the most frightful mess. They do clear it up afterwards (to a certain extent), but while the work is in progress and the mess is being created I suffer from disturbing emotions. I feel as if I have lost control over an area of my life for which I have overwhelming responsibility. I get a strong urge either to check and fuss and supervise, or to tell them to leave it all to me. In other words I experience difficulty in letting go. If I give in to these feelings and start getting them to do things my way, they would soon become demotivated and I would be left on my own in the kitchen, and it would serve me right.

People need to do things their way, and to feel 'ownership' of the tasks in order to be motivated. When we suffer from the difficulty of letting go of the 'ownership' of the home scene we become bad at managing our domestic helpers and at delegating to them.

I am often astonished at the domestic involvement of men when they are on a boating or camping holiday. Men, and their sons, who often do no housework at home, will sweep floors, clean lavatories, cook and wash up, even if the wife is there to help out. They seem to take responsibility for the housekeeping and are motivated through a sense of ownership. It is because we women do not share our domestic power and ownership at home that we get lumbered with all of the responsibility and most of the tasks.

NEGOTIATING HELP

In my household, I have bought my way out of doing domestic chores. I have a mother's help and a cleaner, and between them they do nearly everything I would do if I were a housewife rather than a career woman. This saves me a great deal of time and effort but it doesn not completely solve the problem. Hindered by conditioning that tells me that the household and children are *my* responsibility, I have never negotiated a share of that responsibility with my husband. When things go wrong and the home help fails because of holidays or illness, it is *my* work which takes second place in the panic to wash clothes and take children to school.

Recently a domestic crisis arose because the home help failed during the school holidays. I had a tough three weeks, and only by exploiting my network and using my organisational skills to the full was I able to survive the period without losing a client. I was a nervous wreck at the end and one day I exploded at my husband, told him how difficult I had found the experience, and said how mean he was to have left me to sort it all out. He was bewildered. *'You never asked me to do anything,'* he said. And that was true. When I calmed down we discussed it and I realised that if we had examined the problem together at the start we could have worked out a sensible way of sharing the work!

The biggest block of all to rationality at home is a highly-charged emotional problem. One woman expresses it very clearly.

Cooking and providing a home is one way of showing love. When, because of other pressures, I didn't want to do these things *my husband felt I didn't love him.*

In many families the children and husband feel loved and cared for because they have someone to look after them physically. This means that women may be inhibited from delegating this care to someone else, because it can seem as if we are withdrawing our love.

So, for a whole number of reasons to do with how we see our roles as women, we may find it hard to organise our home life in a way which is consistent with having a successful career. It is interesting that while many women have decided to challenge traditional stereotypes of women by having careers and taking jobs in a male world, some of us still back away from challenging them at home. While we are ready to become solicitors and managers, we still feel a need to don our aprons and plug in our vacuum cleaners at home.

What can we do about this problem? Obviously a full domestic role does not go hand-in-hand with a busy, senior role at work. Even if we are not yet at the top, the decks need to be cleared for the effort of getting there. But there are a number of ways in which we can confront our conditioning and take some practical steps towards improving the situation. Don't be discouraged if you have some insurmountable obstacles to delegating household management. Even if you can only make small changes it will make a difference. Sometimes we have to bide our time until new opportunities arrive, or until fate plays into our hands (for example, when our children grow up).

CHALLENGING YOUR CONDITIONING

The first step is to confront the traditional view that homemaking means giving love, and if we do less in the home we are giving less love. There *are* other ways of showing love than cooking and cleaning, which are *more* nurturing. Having the energy for sex is one important way. Having the time for a social life with our partners, or just to do things with them and to talk to them is another.

My husband gets upset when, due to a frantic schedule, he feels I have no time to talk to him. He would rather have my company and conversation to a grand meal cooked by a tired wife who falls asleep after dinner. My children like me to play cards or tennis with them in the evenings, and would rather not lose me into the kitchen or behind an ironing board. I now do not feel guilty about delegating household chores, because my family treasure the time I spend having fun with them.

Seeing things this way will help you to let go of some of those strings that kept you tied to the kitchen sink. It also helps if your family or partner sees it this way as well. You may need to discuss it with them and explain that they will benefit as well as you if some of these chores are shared, and that it's because you want to spend more time with them that you want to do less housework.

The second step is to ask yourself these questions:

• What do I want for myself in my personal life?
• What am I not achieving?

When you have a list of your needs, desires and your shortfalls, make another list, this time of all the factors which stop you from achieving what you want. Now is the time to get ruthless. Look at each factor on the list and ask yourself:

- Do I really *have* to do these things?
- What is the conditioning, the inner messages which compel me to do these things?
- To what extent do I contribute to this situation?

Now make a list of the 'inner messages' that govern the way you run your home life. Some of these messages can be very powerful. To give yourself the courage to counter them, try to see the price you are now paying for listening to them. Often it is high.

After this analysis the next step might be to find friends and acquaintances who are doing things differently. Often hearing about the way they cope can give you the inspiration and courage to try it yourself. Let's illustrate this with an example given by one of the women I interviewed. When she asked herself what she wanted in her personal life she realised that she was not achieving some important personal goals. She had little energy to play with her children. Her sex life was deteriorating. She wasn't having any fun. Her health was poor and she was suffering from an increasing number of migraines.

When she listed the factors which stopped her from achieving what she wanted from her personal life she found it all boiled down to tiredness and stress caused by having too much to do. She would come home from working and cook a three-course meal for the three adults in her house. Then she would clear away while the others watched television. Finally, with the help of her doctor, she realised that she was contributing to her own downfall. She looked at all the tasks that filled her day and asked herself if she really had to do these things. Of course she didn't, but her inner messages saying that women do the cooking and clearing up were very powerful. One night she went home and cooked a one-course, stir-fry meal, and nothing else. After dinner she asked her husband to help with the clearing up. Nobody complained, in fact they thought it was quite sensible. Because that experiment worked she had the confidence to reorganise other aspects of her domestic life.

Getting a partner or an older child to do domestic chores when they are accustomed to be waited on by you hand and foot can be difficult. If someone is conditioned by you to sit back while you do all the work, you have to think out a strategy for changing the situation gradually. There's no point (although understandable) having an outburst one night when you're really tired. A low-key request for assistance is more likely to get a favourable response, and won't lead to resentment. Start small and work up to getting them to do a reasonable share.

On the other hand, in some partnerships, it may be appropriate to become more challenging. For whatever reason, some men are downright lazy or irrational about pulling their weight at home. A busy woman journalist had this problem to relate:

Not only does my husband do no housework, but he creates a mess everywhere, he is worse than a child. His clothes and shoes are strewn over every room, and he is incapable of shutting a drawer or cupboard door once he has opened it. If he eats a banana he leaves the peel on the table for me to throw away. The irony is that he is, in some ways, a supporter of women's rights and is very much in favour of women working, including me. I guess he feels that giving emotional support is enough! Well it isn't, and I am now learning ways of getting him to take some responsibility. I think of my needs, and become irresponsible myself when I feel like I need a break. Sometimes I just stay out late and phone him to say that he has to feed our daughter and put her to bed. Occasionally, I arrange a few days in Paris or somewhere nice with a female colleague – half-work, half-fun. I just tell him when I'm going and when I'll be back. I don't baby him by pre-cooking food or making any special arrangments. He copes. I am learning not to feel guilty.

Once *you* begin to accept that the house and family should be a shared responsibility and not only yours, then that's half the battle won.

I used to do all of the housework until we started a family. Now working, mothering and housekeeping is too much for me, something has to give. Under pressure, I began to feel that I was silly to take all of these responsibilities onto my shoulders and the process of training my partner began. I just began to let go under pressure, and housekeeping standards fell, in some cases low enough so that he noticed. 'This shelf is very dirty,' he remarked. 'You know where the dusters are,' I said. 'The dinner plates haven't been cleared away,' was another comment. 'You know how to load the dishwasher. I'm tired tonight.' And slowly but surely he began to either accept the mess without complaint or do something about it himself.

These two stories were told by women in their thirties and forties who are married to what I call the 'ambivalents' – the men who think it's a great idea that women work because it makes them more interesting, but don't want any reduction in the service at home. Many younger women in their twenties are having an easier time of it now. The lucky ones find men who are really committed to the idea of women working, and understand that it means sharing responsibility for domestic matters. But it's still not plain sailing for everyone. Watch out, there are still MCPs about who plan big careers for themselves and want wives who will slave for them so they can concentrate on the race to the top.

If you are a young working woman just starting up a partnership, take note. It's easier to get men to do their bit now in most cases, but make sure you agree a fair division of labour at the start and stick to it. Men are easier to train when they're young and in love. Don't wait until they begin to enjoy putting their feet up at home at your expense, and then try to change them.

PRIORITIES AT WORK AND HOME
When life becomes frantic we have to decide our priorities and plan our time carefully, including time for rest and relaxation. At work we have to plan the use of our time and decide what tasks to put aside when we have a staff shortage or a deadline to meet. We need to get into the habit of using these skills at home. The women I interviewed had all eventually formed the habit of discarding inessential chores when they were under pressure. Elaborate cooking, business entertaining for husbands, tidying up and gardening were the sort of tasks that went by the board. The trick when setting priorities is to keep your long-term personal goals in mind.

It's no good deciding priorities on your own, however, if you have a husband and family whose ideas about what is important might be different. The arts of consulting, discussing and negotiating need to be brought home too.

Choose the right moment and plan your approach. Explain the pressure you're under from doing two jobs and ask them to help you to think of creative solutions. When they resist solutions that involve them in housework or expenditure, explain again that you cannot do it all on you own. Sell the idea to them by showing the benefits to family income if you are released to concentrate harder on your career and thus earn more. Show also the benefits to family fun and social life if you have more energy left over at weekends and evenings. Keep it light but insist that you need a change and their cooperation. Whatever the details of your case, remember that if you do need cooperation, then the best way to gain commitment to a plan of action is to involve them in problem-solving. Use their solutions whenever you can, and show your appreciation of their efforts to help you solve domestic difficulties.

Sometimes you may find that these negotiations get bogged down in subjectivity. 'But I *do* help with the housework. Why, even last week I did the ironing. You make me feel like a monster when I'm not!' If you just say, 'You don't do enough' in response to that, it can harden attitudes. Instead, get some objectivity into the discussion. Draw up a checklist of all the domestic chores, and the time they take, and see how much time each member of the family spends on these things in total. If they see that the total time they spend on chores is only a fraction of the time you spend, they may begin to see the light.

Use this checklist as a guide.

Activity	Time		
	Him	Her	Children
Cooking: Breakfast			
Lunch			
Dinner			
Washing up (or loading the dishwasher)			
Unloading the dishwasher			
Vacuuming			
Dusting			
Cleaning bathrooms and lavatories			

Activity	Time		
	Him	Her	Children
Renewing loo rolls			
Renewing soap and toothpaste			
Cleaning mirrors			
Cleaning windows			
Feeding animals			
Grooming animals			
Spring cleaning			
Cleaning the cooker			
Cleaning the kitchen floor			
Washing			
Ironing			
Changing sheets			
Making beds			
Household shoppping			
Polishing brass or silver			
Taking clothes to the cleaners			
Changing light bulbs			
Decorating			
Changing plugs			
Mending broken machines			
Mowing the lawn			
Gardening			
Cleaning the car(s)			
Taking the car to be serviced			
Dealing with personal finances			
Staying at home so people can get in to fix things			
Feeding children			
Getting up in the night to deal with children			
Changing nappies			
Bathing children			
Taking children to the doctor/dentist			
Organising schooling and extra-curricular activities			
Helping children with homework			

Activity	Time		
	Him	Her	Children
Going to school events			
Ferrying children around			
Organising social life			
Writing thank you letters			
Making the fire			
Cleaning the fireplace			
Cleaning shoes			
Moving house			
Planning holidays			

This list is probably endless. Just delete the irrelevant and add any missing items. If you have a cleaner, housekeeper or nanny doing some of these chores, then use the checklist for the chores that are left over.

CRISIS MANAGEMENT

However carefully we plan and organise our lives there will be times when we are faced with a crisis. Whether the pipes have burst, the washing machine has broken down or the mother's help has walked out on you, clear-thinking, problem-solving and action-planning skills are needed.

First of all think about the management of crises at work and try to apply these principles at home. Most well-run establishments have back-up manual systems in case their automated systems fail. They also have alternative suppliers, staff agencies, temporary workers etc. Make sure that you have supplies of food in your freezer, and a microwave oven in case of a cooking disaster just before a big family dinner. To cover child minder illnesses or walk-outs, a whole network of friends and relatives is necessary. People like to help out in crises, as long as you don't ask them too regularly. If you're always having a crisis you'll soon begin to lose sympathy. Some agencies are better at supplying help at short notice than others. Find out which these are *before* disaster strikes. One of the women I interviewed took the trouble years ago to teach her husband to cook, now if she suddenly has to entertain when she is very busy he can take over.

In a well-run office, teamwork is often at its best in a crisis. Everyone pulls together. See if you can generate team spirit the next time you have a crisis at home, with everyone suggesting how to *solve* the problem and what tasks they can do.

ENTERTAINING

Home entertaining can be a problem for a busy working woman. Often the extra pressure takes the pleasure out of the occasion. Yet we need our friends and helpful relatives. To maintain these important networks we often need to entertain. How can we make it easier? Challenge those inner messages that tell us we have to do it all ourselves, and do it the hard way. Ask yourself what your friends would prefer, a cheerful, vivacious you, or great food. If providing marvellous food all on your own means you're too tired to enjoy the event and be splendid company, then ask yourself if you have got your priorities right.

The women I interviewed had all decided that their main priority was to enjoy the event themselves, and this goal determined the way they approached their entertaining.

When I am having people to dinner I prepare over three days before so that I don't ignore the children and cause problems on the day of the party, and so that I am not too exhausted to entertain.

Some who can afford to, use outside caterers. Those who cannot, make other decisions to simplify their preparation when under pressure. One now cooks simple, healthy food instead of elaborate menus as she did in the past. Others say they use good quality pre-prepared food or will take their guests out for a curry. Usually people admire busy women who find ways of conserving their energy so that they can be entertaining.

My experience with using caterers and pre-prepared food is that everyone assumes you have cooked it yourself. When faced with compliments over a delicious meal and remarks about what a good cook you are, just smile and say 'thank you'.

174

SHOPPING

Friday evenings and Saturdays are the times when the busy working woman needs to have some fun and relaxation to recover from the tensions of the week. Instead, what do we do? We pour into the crowded supermarkets in our thousands. What a way to end the week! Is it really necessary to shop every week, at peak times, and to do it all yourself?

It is not necessary to go to the supermarket every week. Try going once a month and fill several trolleys with shopping, so you're well stocked up.

See how much of your shopping could be delivered. I discovered that the butcher delivered bulk orders of meat, the milkman delivered eggs, yoghurts, bread and fruit juice, and greengrocers delivered fruit, vegetables and flowers! There was no charge for any of these deliveries and they cut my shopping time down to a fraction of what it had been.

Try gettting your older children, husband or mother's help to do some of your shopping. At first they may make mistakes but you can train them over time by giving them lists with quantities and preferred substitutes. The pay-off in time and energy saved is so great that it is worth the risk of having to put up with the wrong cooking oil and pink lavatory paper!

DEALING WITH MEN AT HOME

Do you use your people handling skills at home when you're negotiating with decorators, repair men etcetera? Do you use your full authority and power with tradesmen who challenge the ability of a woman to make certain decisions? Many women are not good at this. Because we have the option to hide behind the strong backs of our husbands or partners we often do exactly that. How often do you hear yourself saying, 'I have to discuss this with my husband first.'

One of my interviewees used to say, 'My husband wouldn't like it' to errant tradesmen who were inclined to be chauvinistic and to challenge her authority. Then one day a carpenter suggested phoning her husband first to get his permission to do some work she had instructed him to do. She blew up. After that she got into the habit of using her own authority, not her husband's.

Workmen, tradesmen and decorators may not expect authority and decisiveness from a woman, but they recognise it when they see it. If you find them treating you with contempt, ask yourself, 'Is it because I am a woman, or is it because of my behaviour?' Don't let them bully or manipulate you into hasty, poor decisions. If you need time to think or to get more information, say so. If you want to compare prices or service with a competitor, say so. They will then realise they are dealing with someone they have to respect. Practise saying, 'I have decided,' rather than, 'My husband has decided.' Once you get into the habit of using your authority and standing by your decisions you will become more effective at dealing with anyone who comes to your front door.

The theme of this chapter has been that the busy working woman can organise her domestic life so that there is time for enjoyment and pleasure. But a big gain is that it will enable her to realise her full potential at work. If you are still reluctant to change your domestic practices, then maybe you need to take one more look at those inner messages I have been speaking about. Could it be that you are hiding behind your domestic responsibilities and using them as an excuse for low achievement at work? Are you scared that if you removed your excuses you still wouldn't climb to the top? The challenges of growth and development are frightening, but the rewards for facing up to these challenges are enormous.

11

Combining motherhood with a career

Most of the women I interviewed did not have children. Those who did either worked for themselves, or took long career breaks when their children were young. It is still very difficult to combine a senior job with motherhood. Babies tend to come at a time – late twenties to mid thirties – when you need to focus on your job and work hard if you are going to get anywhere near the top. If you work for yourself, motherhood need not hold you back from success. But if you work for someone else it can threaten your career progress. Faced with this knowledge, young women have to make decisions that men don't have to face:

- Not to have children and hope to gain fulfilment from a successful career.

Or

- Have children and stop working or remain stuck in jobs that don't use their full potential.

PLANNING FOR MOTHERHOOD

For this chapter I interviewed the few women I know who have managed to get into senior positions in their organisations at the same time as bringing children into the world. One of these is Jacky Woodhouse who has two young boys and a senior job with Prudential Insurance. Jacky is an inspiration to many of the younger women in her company as she has successfully weathered the storms associated with rearing small children and now many of these other women feel they could do it too, if they chose to. Jacky's choice was not an easy one, but she made it work by planning her way carefully and by being sensitive to the problems her motherhood caused for the people she works with.

Another case is Pauline Buchanan Black, who is director of the London Housing Association's training scheme. Pauline has a young son and has continued to work at her busy job. Although she is very senior, she is not highly paid because she works in the voluntary sector. Her success at combining work with motherhood also relied on careful planning.

I hope that through reading about the experiences of these career mothers, women will find it easier to decide whether they wish to travel that route. If they do decide to have children I also hope that this chapter will help them to plan their motherhood in a way which makes it possible to be successful, both as a career woman and as a mother.

SHALL I OR SHAN'T I?

The first hurdle is deciding whether to have children or not. Jacky Woodhouse didn't feel strongly about having children, but was pressurised by her mother to do so. Although Jacky didn't feel a strong desire to have children she is very glad she made the decision.

> Not only do I get a great kick out of having their company, but I can't help thinking how much better my old age will be for having children. It gives me something to look forward to. Otherwise old age could be pretty empty and lonely. It's nice to have someone to live for other than yourself. It gives you a stake in the future.

For other women, engrossed in their careers, the pressures

may come from their husbands. Alternatively, as we enter our thirties the biological clock starts to point at twilight and we feel that it's now or never.

This is how one successful woman in her thirties feels:

> I am thirty-three now and I have to ask myself – am I going to have children? I don't want to have any! I don't want my relationship with my husband to change. We're very happy. It's such an irrevocable decision. For the first time in my life I am wishing I were a man. I would want a break of two years if I had a baby and my career would certainly suffer. I can think of lots of reasons against having children. I think I would be an appalling mother. I'm so bossy. If I had a son I might bring him up to be the sort of man I despise! My parents assumed I would give up work when I got married. This acts as an incentive for me not to do so! Yet I feel the old biological clock ticking away – I am *very* aware of it.

Another senior woman in her early forties feels that successful women fall into a trap which tricks them into not having children.

> If you're going to be successful, your career tends to take off in your late twenties and early thirties. You mature then, become able to deal with people, and begin to be taken seriously. This happens at the same time that we begin to wonder if we should have kids. There is so much risk and uncertainty around having children. If you're having a great time at work it's tempting just to carry on enjoying yourself.

The decision whether to have children or not, and when, can be made more easily by facing up to the reality of your circumstances. Ask yourself these sorts of questions:

- Do I want children at all? Would I be happy to go through life without having any?
- Do I have a job which makes motherhood *and* success at all possible? If you have a job which demands of you that you work fourteen hours a day, or that you jet round the world and are rarely at home, then child-rearing could be a problem.
- Do I have a husband who is willing and able to share some of the motherhood role? If you are away from home a lot but your

husband's job permits him to come home quite early most evenings, then this can be an alternative to having you there all the time – as long as he is a willing party to this arrangement.

- Do I have some practical child care options? Practical child care usually means one of three things. You either need willing relatives who live close by; a reputable, reliable child minder; or to be able to afford a nanny. Sometimes nannies can be shared with other mothers, thus lessening the bill, but this does depend on a lot of luck.

If you cannot answer these questions positively, then having children will interrupt your career. Maybe you need to wait until your circumstances change, or until you have established yourself sufficiently to afford a nanny.

A young information technologist I know has just had a baby and is determined to carry on working. She can't afford a nanny's salary all on her own, so she has been very creative about making child care arrangements. For the first month she was at home with her baby, she made sure that he saw a lot of her mother and sister. Then, as she got a bit busier, she got a child minder to help out on some days. As a result of this, the baby is quite happy to spend his time with people other than her. Now that she is returning to work full-time, she is going to share a nanny with a friend who lives close by, who also has a baby. Not only does it make it cheaper, but it is probably nicer for the babies as well.

I had two children while working as an employee for a management consultancy company. My job involved a great deal of travelling and I was often away from home all week. I did have excellent child care arrangements but was unrealistic about trying to combine motherhood with a travelling job. The senior managers in the company were uncomfortable with the situation and when I was on maternity leave with my second baby I was made redundant. This motivated me to set up my own business, which certainly made motherhood a lot easier to manage. However, the fact remains that my career as a full-time employee was interrupted because I did have a job which was difficult to combine with motherhood. On the other hand, if working for yourself is a real option, having a career break will not hold you back from ultimate success in the way it can do if you work for someone else.

Jacky Woodhouse's circumstances were different. She had a

job which could be combined with motherhood, and working hours that enabled her to be home by 6.30 most evenings. She was already doing well at work and could afford a nanny, and her husband is able to be at home by 6.30 on those evenings she has to work late.

Nonetheless, it was a courageous thing to do. Jacky was one of the first women to make it into management in a company which was very male dominated. She was breaking new ground and had no models to follow.

MATERNAL DEPRIVATION

Another problem which can hold a career woman back from having children, even if her circumstances are favourable, is the concern over maternal deprivation. Many people still believe that a young child needs its mother around all the time, and will suffer personality problems if she is missing for some of the time. If you feel this to be the case then it would be a mistake to try to work when your children are young. Your guilt feelings would interfere with your performance at work and at home. It would be better to have a break and accept that it may harm your career. Don't think that it's the end of your prospects if you take that decision as when you do finally return to work feeling ready to carry on with your career, you will find that your more positive attitude will pay dividends. Carrying on with your job when you have babies at home by no means guarantees success. It can be a time when a woman's career progression slows down anyway, because she can't throw herself wholeheartedly into her job.

For those career women who are unsure about the issue of maternal deprivation it is worth examining the facts so that they can make an informed decision about having children. Betty Friedan in her book *The Feminine Mystique* was the first to expose maternal deprivation as a myth. The statistics available in the 1960s showed that the children of working mothers did not seem to be disadvantaged in any way. On the contrary, the psychological problems were suffered by the children of non-working mothers who tried to live their lives through their offspring, thus smothering them and inhibiting their emotional growth. The children of working mothers tend to be more independent. The issue, I think, is not whether the mother is around all the time, but whether someone who loves the child is around all or most of the time. Thus, fathers, grandmothers or child minders can give the child the nurturing it needs. It is the quality of time a mother spends with her offspring that is important, not the quantity. If she gives her child a gratifying amount of love and attention when she is with him or her, the child should be emotionally healthy, and able to cope with her absences.

Maternal deprivation is more likely to be experienced when a child does not have a love object to nurture it for most of the day. This can happen at nurseries when each attendant has many children to care for, and cannot develop a close, special, loving relationship with any individual child. It can also happen if the child minder neglects the child or does not love it.

So, if you are thinking about having a child, but worried about caring for it, then take heart from women who do successfully combine motherhood with careers. As long as they manage the care of their children so that someone loving is around, then those children will not suffer. In fact, these children may have many advantages. They will tend to be more independent. They will also have the benefit of a relationship with a mother who is fulfilled and getting all she can out of life. Often the extra self-confidence and sense of purpose that a career woman displays makes her a good model for her children.

Jacky Woodhouse does not feel that her children are deprived because she works. In fact she knows that being a working mother is the best thing for her and her children.

> Had I been at home I would have driven them 'potty'. I am such a strong personality that I would have 'cramped their style'! My absence during the day gives them an opportunity to develop as individuals.

Although she does feel that what is right for her is not necessarily right for others.

PART-TIME OPTIONS
There is another option to having a career break. That is to work part-time when your children are very young, instead of giving up work completely for a few years. This can often be easier to arrange than finding full-time child minders. I know many women who found that this worked well for them. They

discovered that having a part-time job gave them the intellectual stimulation and adult company that they needed without separating them from their children for too long each week.

As an option for a woman who is serious about her career however, it also brings frustrations. Part-time pay is usually low, and it is difficult to progress your career and get to do more challenging work unless you are full-time. However, it does keep your foot in the door, and your confidence levels up. It also looks impressive on your CV, making future prospective employers feel that you are serious about your career, and that you have up-to-date and relevant experience.

There is another factor you should consider if you are trying to decide whether to have a career break when your babies arrive, or to carry on working. Women who spend a few years at home with their children sometimes find that when they eventually go back to work it is very disconcerting, even traumatic, for their children. A child who has become accustomed to having its mother around all the time will often find it hard suddenly to have to do without her for a large part of every day. It doesn't happen in every case, but I know several mothers who have had to struggle through months, or even years, of tearful, clingy children who are not happy with the alternative child care arrangements. Having to part from a distraught child every morning can weaken your resolve to continue with your career. And it's not very nice for the child either!

Although carrying on with the job when your children are babies has its own problems, one advantage is that your children become accustomed at an early age to having their mother come and go. To these children it's simply how things are – my children take it in their stride. They have three adults who take care of them: the mother's help, their father and their mother, and they were always with one or other of these much-loved people when they were young. As a result of this early conditioning my children never felt deserted when I set off in the morning. They have a good, loving relationship with me, but not an intense, over-dependent one which makes them feel they could not do without me. The only times when things went wrong, and they were unhappy, were the two occasions when I recruited unsuitable mother's helps. As soon as I realised what was happening I changed the mother's help and matters quickly settled down again.

If you decide to take a career break then there is a way round this problem, but you must plan for it. You need to work out how you are going to raise your children so that they will be able to cope with your absences when you return to work – perhaps by getting them to spend time with other adults when they are quite young. Friends or relatives who live close by may be willing to help, especially if you reciprocate with their children.

FATHERCARE

Another child-minding option that some women are finding nowadays, is that the *father* may want to spend a lot of his time with his children. It is still unusual, and men doing this can suffer from role reversal problems, but don't rule it out if your partner has the time and inclination. Fathers can make very good mothers!

TIMING

If you decide to have a child *and* keep your job, then the next thing to consider is the timing of your pregnancy. By 'timing' I don't mean what month of the year you wish to start your pregnancy, because it is usually difficult to achieve such close control of the process. When I decided to have a baby I aimed to give birth in January. A year-and-a-half later I was still trying to conceive! Timing is more about the stage in your career when you would find the pregnancy least disruptive. A client of mine had decided to have a baby a few weeks before getting an important promotion. She was then in her late twenties and opted to wait for two years so that she could establish herself in her new job before having to take a short break. She felt that her credibility as a serious career woman would be damaged if she announced her pregnancy a few months after the promotion.

Jacky Woodhouse had her two children at a time in her career when the organisation could afford to lose her for a few months. Now that she is working at a higher management level her day-to-day responsibilities are such that she would find it difficult to take a break. However, she had her babies before she got up to that level.

BREAKING THE NEWS

Once you become pregnant the next issue is how to break the news at work. Most women wait until after the first three months because the chances of miscarriage in that initial period are quite high. I waited until I was five months pregnant to tell my boss, but by that time he had already guessed, so I should have told him sooner! The big problem is that it can be hard to get people to believe that you really intend to return to work. So many women say they will and then decide to stay at home that there is a certain amount of cynicism around about this issue.

Jacky discovered the same attitude. She took her boss out to lunch and told him of her plans, and she could see that he did not believe she would return. She then broke the news personally to her boss's boss. Finally, by being very persistent, she convinced her boss that he had to plan for her short maternity leave.

In order to get people at work to take her career plans seriously Jacky did a number of things:

- She worked until five days before the baby was born.
- She arranged for all of her correspondence to be sent to her home while she was on maternity leave.
- She was on the telephone to the office a week after the baby was born.
- She worked at home while she was on maternity leave for about ten to fifteen hours a week.

By the time she returned to work after three months everyone had realised that she seriously intended to continue with her career.

RETURNING TO WORK

Returning to work after having a baby can be difficult. The extra levels of hormones in your body, and then their withdrawal, cause some psychological changes. Also, having a baby is a big shock to the system, both physically and emotionally. It is hard to predict exactly how you will feel afterwards. The best approach is to be aware that there may be some irrational feelings, although you won't be able to predict what form they will take, and how they will affect your behaviour.

The particular emotional problem that Jacky found was that she experienced 'a total lack of confidence' the minute she walked back into the company. These feelings lasted for the first month and then subsided. She did not reveal her anxieties to anyone, but she did ask a subordinate to check all her work before sending it out. She was also very tired and life felt like a struggle for the first three months back at her job. In retrospect she realises that she may have returned too soon, but she had been so aware of the need to get back to work that she never stopped to consider her stamina.

Some women go back to work a few weeks after having a baby, but this may be counterproductive. It will show that you are serious about your career, but your performance may be so poor because of the stress and tiredness that it may do more to damage your image than a longer break. It is hard to imagine the emotional and physical consequences of having a baby until you have had one. These consequences will vary with each individual, but they will always be significant. Young women may bounce back relatively quickly, but most career women have their children in their thirties. By this age you can guarantee that as a minimum you will find it very tiring, however joyous!

I can still remember how exhausted I felt all the time when my children were young. I would stand at the back steps of the house at the end of the day and survey their toys strewn all over the garden and think, 'Where am I going to get the energy from to clear that lot up and to give them their baths?' Somehow I found it, but life was tough. I often had to work away from home in those days, teaching on residential management courses. I used to arrive at these courses, breathe a sigh of relief and say, 'Ah, now I can relax for five days and get some sleep!' The two other trainers I worked with would stare at me in amazement. 'How can a high-pressure management course be more relaxing than life at home with two lovely children?' they would exclaim. A few years later they both started their own families and now they know exactly what I meant!

ORGANISATION

There are not only emotional adjustments to face when you return to work after a baby. There are also organisational problems. Combining a career with motherhood plunges you into years of planning and organising. When things go smoothly and the children and the child minder are well and happy, it seems like a simple operation that anyone could manage but when disaster strikes it can seem like the end of the world. To make it worse, in the early years of motherhood, people at work will be watching you to see if you can really manage the dual role.

Jacky has had her fair share of organisational problems. Two weeks after returning to work after her second baby the nanny left. Jacky's aim, as far as work was concerned, was to avoid suddenly absenting herself without warning. She managed not to do this by getting help from her in-laws and her husband. She was therefore in a position to say, 'I am going to need three days off in a week's time', and this caused no problem at work. She never had to phone up in the morning and say, 'I can't make it today'.

THE EMOTIONAL PROBLEMS

It would be misleading to suggest that managing children and jobs is only about getting on top of organisational problems. When things go wrong (and they will) it's not just an inconvenience, it can make you very fraught and unhappy.

Here are some emotional problems faced by working mothers:

When things go wrong with the children, I feel like such a failure. I have the most awful thoughts bubbling up inside of me like – I should never have had these kids in the first place, it wasn't fair to lumber them with such a rotten mother! Sometimes I come home tired from work and I snap at one and he starts to cry. I could kill myself. I get the nanny to take them to the health clinic when I'm too busy to take time off. I found out this year that somehow the youngest had failed to get the last in a series of crucial injections. I guess it happened because I wasn't there all the time to ensure continuity. I over react, but I feel so guilty I can't help myself.

When one of the children is sick it's an awful strain. Once I was running a conference and my three-year-old got a chest infection. My mother-in-law came over to babysit because I couldn't leave the conference. I telephoned home seven or eight times each day. The child had a high fever and it wouldn't go down. Every time I telephoned, it was the same bad news. At night I slept with her, and one night she was delirious. I didn't sleep a wink. She lost weight because she couldn't eat and ended up looking like a stick insect. Finally, after four days of this, she began to get better. I was a wreck. I just broke down and cried when I saw how thin she was. I too caught the infection and ended up with bronchitis. It just had to happen. The stress made me ill.

There are other organisational problems:

- What happens when you want to take them to school on their first day and it clashes with a command invitation from the chairman to attend a meeting?
- What happens when you're late home from the office and you've only got twenty minutes with your child before going out to dinner? It's easy enough to say, 'If the child is happy, go on out with a light heart, and if she is unhappy, turn up late to the dinner.' It's the guilt and the pulls from so many directions that dig into your heart.

There is no magic solution to these emotional horrors. You will face them on and off all through motherhood. And the problems never completely go away because your children will probably want you to be a good grandmother!

There are two things that you need to do to hold on to your sanity:

- Try to encourage and allow the father to be a good mother too.
- Don't feel you have to be perfect. Stay-at-home mothers aren't perfect either. All you need to be to raise emotionally healthy children is a *good enough* mother, not the best.

All working mothers have to make contingency plans to cope with such pressures. Jacky's strength is that her husband feels a responsibility to share the problem and is willing to take time off himself. She also has relatives to whom she can turn. She plans her diary well in advance so that she can take leave for known activities involving the children, like school concerts and birthday parties etc.

Like all working mothers, Jacky had to cope with the problem of guilt. Even though we know our children are being loved and nurtured by someone else, it is difficult to avoid pangs of guilt because we can't be with them all the time. Jacky acknowledged her feelings and decided to be with her baby every minute she was not in the office. She would never go away for the weekend without the baby, she felt she needed a few hours alone with the baby on Saturdays and Sundays for her own emotional nurturance. Even though she had these emotions she felt that being a working mother was what she wanted. When the second child came along Jacky took six months maternity leave and loved having that interlude to spend with her children. When she went back to work after her second baby she was less tired.

By her careful organisation Jacky established a reputation for being serious about combining motherhood with a career, and is a marvellous example of what can be achieved.

However, she found that in spite of this she was not progressing as fast as she hoped in the early years of motherhood. She stayed at the same level for five years until, prompted by an offer from a headhunter, she confronted her bosses with the apparent stagnation in her career. To her surprise, she learnt that she had been left at her level because it had been assumed that, on becoming a mother, that was where she wanted to remain. She wrote a letter to her boss putting the record straight on her career ambitions. Within six months she was promoted.

We all have to be aware of the danger that our managers may make the assumption, in spite of evidence to the contrary, that we, as mothers, need a job which is not too demanding. No matter how well we organise our personal lives, these assumptions will be made. It is up to us to tell them otherwise. If you are lucky enough to have a boss who has a working wife, then you may not experience this problem. Many managers, however, will have wives who stay at home with their children. These men will have trouble realising that it is possible to do otherwise and may harm your career in their well-intentioned effort to make things easy for you.

DEALING WITH DISAPPROVAL

Jacky has had to put up with the usual remarks from people at work who disapprove of mothers working. One of the senior, male managers raised the subject in the management dining room. When he learnt that Jacky had two children at home he said, 'I think that's disgusting!' The whole table listened in silence as Jacky discussed the issue. She kept calm, did not raise her voice, respected his point of view, and stated what she thought was right. In this way she prevented the problem from escalating and won the respect of the manager concerned. Jacky feels that what she is doing is right and gathers strength from the conviction.

OVERCOMING PREJUDICE

So few women combine raising children with senior jobs that each one of us starting on that route has to prove herself afresh. Jacky finds that when she is trying to persuade her colleagues to believe in the seriousness of the career ambitions of other women in her organisation she often meets with the usual prejudice against women. When she says, 'But look here, *I* did it,' she gets the reply, 'But you're different!' These prejudices make it harder, but they don't make it impossible. The point is we have to learn from the few pioneers about the sorts of problems and obstacles we will have to face, and organise ourselves to overcome them.

PAULINE BUCHANAN BLACK'S EXPERIENCE

Pauline Buchanan Black did not consider having children until she was in her middle thirties and living happily with a very supportive partner. She did not want to have children earlier on, mainly because she never felt she wanted to start a family with her first husband.

When Pauline decided that she wanted a child, many of the circumstances were right. She did work in a low-paid sector of the economy, but because she had a senior job which paid that little bit more, and a partner with a steady income, she could afford to pay someone to look after her baby while she was at work. This was an important consideration because she had no relatives living near to her in London who could have helped with child minding. She had a demanding job, but one that was flexible enough to allow her to take work home in the evenings when she had to be back for babysitting. Her partner was supportive and keen to become a father, and also able to come home early some days of the week to enable Pauline to work late. She did some travelling, but not a great deal.

Pauline knew that there was never going to be a good time for taking maternity leave from her job, so she waited until she and her partner had found a suitable house and then got pregnant.

DELEGATION

Even before she became pregnant, Pauline began to develop some of her staff through delegation and training so that she would be able to leave them in charge while she was on maternity leave. This was good management practice on her part anyway, since her staff became less dependent on her.

When Pauline became pregnant she had a plan all worked out for coping with her maternity leave before she told the management committee who were her employers. She told them how the office would be run in her absence, who would do what, and how they would be financially compensated for taking on extra responsibilities. She felt she had to do this to show that she wasn't 'just a silly woman who would leave them in the lurch'. She managed this well, and when she broke the news her employers believed she would be coming back to work, because of her planning and because they knew how committed she was to the organisation.

Pauline made her announcement in 1987, several years after Jacky made hers. So many more women are now returning to work after having babies that it is probably getting easier to convince your employers that you mean to do that yourself. It is essential that they believe you, because an absence of three or four months does require some serious planning.

Pauline was faced with a mountain of organisational work to prepare the office for her absence. Fortunately her pregnancy was a healthy one and she was able to work hard until her maternity leave started, a month before the baby came.

BEING INFLUENTIAL WHEN YOU'RE PREGNANT
One issue which Pauline had to worry about was how to influence people when she was obviously pregnant. She had no difficulty with her staff and bosses who knew her and believed in her. The potential problem was with clients from outside the organisation. All of her dealings with these people were carried out over the telephone, so she resolved the issue by asking her staff to keep her pregnancy a secret. Her clients couldn't see her, so they didn't worry.

(I had no such luck when I was pregnant. All of my client dealings were face-to-face – or tummy-to-tummy as I got bigger. It was a problem. I could see that many people just didn't want to start projects with me because they didn't believe I would return to work. But I persisted in getting down to business and avoided the trap of being sidetracked by references to my impending motherhood.)

One plus factor is that the extra hormones do tend to make you more placid and easy-going. So what you lose in sharpness and power, you might gain in approachability. I've seen motherhood turn a few women into better managers because it's softened them up and made them more human. Babies can have the same effect on men, although if they don't get involved with their children it may not happen.

ANTE-NATAL CARE

Pauline's main difficulties were at the ante-natal clinic! Here she suddenly found herself in a new world where she was not a respected professional. She was appalled at being kept waiting for up to three hours, and at the inefficiency at the hospital. Her attempts at behaving like a normal, assertive career woman, asking for information and expressing problems, met with failure, indeed with attempts to put her down for being anything other than passive. Trying to assert yourself lying down while being intimately examined, with your tummy sticking out and your skirt up around your neck, is a challenge to any woman. Pauline felt at a disadvantage, surrounded by people who had so much more knowledge about pregnancy and childbirth, and who knew how the system worked. Any woman travelling down this path needs to prepare herself by getting as much information as possible, both by reading and by talking to friends who have had babies.

Pauline returned to work three months after her baby was born. By this time she had recruited a live-in nanny, who started work a few weeks before Pauline did.

NANNY MANAGEMENT

I think it is worth saying something about nanny management because it is a choice that a growing number of career mothers are making today. A recent estimate in *The Times* suggested that over 100,000 families in this country employ nannies. No longer are nannies confined to privileged families. Many middle-income families are finding that they are better off employing a nanny so that the mother can keep her job. Even if you work part-time and don't earn much more than you pay the nanny, it can be worth doing it to keep up your experience in a fast-changing field, so that later, when the children are older, you can start climbing up the ladder again.

Pauline worked out that a live-in nanny was easier for her to afford. Daily nannies need salaries to cover their rent and in a big city this can make them too expensive for middle-income families. She advertised in *The Lady*, that magazine which is the centre of the nanny-employing world. Don't think that if you are not rich and do not live in a beautiful house you cannot attract a nanny. Pauline had several replies to her advertisement and was able to be selective. It is essential before you take on a child minder that you work out the qualities you need in this person, and also the factors that would put you off. Many of these nanny selection criteria will be very personal to you and will depend on what you consider to be important. However, some of the criteria will be important to all mothers trying to raise emotionally healthy children. These were Pauline's criteria.

- Previous experience with a new baby.
- Some professional training.
- Willing to go along with *Pauline's* ideas on child raising.
- Energetic and willing to play with the baby and be concerned with its development.
- Someone who keeps in touch with her family.

Pauline considers it very important that the nanny is not overworked. If you have an overtired or resentful nanny the baby will suffer.

But if *you* are overtired and resentful the baby will also suffer. You need to negotiate a fair arrangement with the nanny. I met a barrister once who had a young baby and she looked so exhausted that I asked her how her babyminding arrangements were working out.

It's awful! I have a nanny, but all she does is look after the baby. I have to wash and iron her clothes as well as mine *and* do all the cooking, which includes feeding her in the evening. I also do the housework, such as it is. She feeds the baby at lunchtime but she doesn't wash up. I have to do that when I come home.

I managed to persuade this woman that she had a rotten deal, and she went away determined to get a more co-operative nanny. The biggest problem with delegating child care is the worry that the nanny (or child minder) will neglect or harm the child. Pauline did have a scare over this. One day, when she was at work, her cleaner telephoned to say that she felt the nanny was neglecting the baby and leaving him to cry a lot. Pauline could think of nothing else all day and wanted to rush home and confront the nanny immediately. However, she decided to discuss it with her partner first and they worked out a way to speak to the nanny about it without having a bust-up. This solved the problem.

When Pauline first went back to work after being away for three months she had a lot to catch up with. Her confidence was undermined at first because there was so much that she didn't know, and she was expected to get back in charge right away. She had to learn to laugh at her predicament, and she shared these feelings with her staff, going through weeks of asking questions before making what had in the past been easy decisions.

Pauline does not feel that her career has suffered since she became a mother. On the contrary, when she returned to work she reorganised the office and increased her staff and, as a result, her salary went up by 25 per cent. However, having a young baby at home has affected her career decision-making for the present. She is now not interested in applying for other, better paid jobs in the organisation which could develop her a lot. She fears that these jobs would interfere with her life style which is focused on giving her an adequate amount of time with her baby and her partner. Interestingly, her partner has made similar career decisions since he became a father. Having two incomes enables this partnership to create a life style which fits well with raising a family. Pauline thinks that when her son is older she may feel differently about taking on more demanding jobs.

When I interviewed her she was looking good. Her baby was nearly a year old and at the tiring stage. She told me that she would never have thought it possible to exist and perform on so little sleep. I could see the tiredness round her eyes but she was alert and firing on all cylinders. Her face was full of life and she looked as if she was doing what she had chosen to do with her life, and liking it.

Both Jacky and Pauline have had to work extra hard to combine motherhood and their careers, yet neither regrets what they have chosen to do. They are both finding their personal lives and their careers rewarding.

WILL IT SERIOUSLY HARM THE CHILDREN?

When you decide to work your way through motherhood, it's very hard not to feel that you are conducting an experiment with precious human lives. Whenever my children are unhappy or doing badly at school I can't help wondering if it would have been better had I stayed at home with them. I know these feelings are irrational, but until a lot more mothers have taken this route and proved that it works, I think many of us will have these little doubts.

When I do find a working mother whose children are grown up and thriving, I am always encouraged. One such person is Esther Denham who became a vet in the 1940s. She was ahead of her times in being determined to have both children and a career. She had four children, and became one of the country's leading vets.

She worked very hard, but admits to being a workaholic. She had to give up her job after her first pregnancy because that's how things were in those days. But about six months later she got an au pair and went back to work. She took less time off with each subsequent child.

Esther loved her children and spent as much time as possible with them. She taught them to play bridge and chess because she thought that was good for them mentally. The four children are grown up now and are doing very well. They have good jobs and are doing what they want to do with their lives. They don't seem to have suffered from having such a hard-working mother. And the nice thing is that Esther's relationship with them is very good. She worked, and she sent them to boarding school, yet there is no lack of closeness in the family. The children all keep in touch and visit their parents regularly.

My advice to anyone who wants to have a baby and keep her job is this: it's possible, but difficult. Be prepared to plan, organise and crisis-manage for the next decade at least, and learn what you can from how other women are managing. It sounds like hard work, and it is. But remember, what people often forget to tell you is that having children is great fun and tremendously rewarding.

References

Key to Footnotes

1. *The Sunday Times*, 24 July 1988.
   'Women knocking at boardroom doors', by Godfrey Golzen.
2. *The Observer*, 6 March, 1988.
   'Chasing men's pay', by Joanna Slaughter.
3. *The Times*, 25 January 1988.
   'Increase in women employees fails to close earnings gap'.
4. *The Globe and Mail* (Canada), 26 March 1987.
   'What women earn.'
5. Adapted from Joan Bardwick's article in Sargent, Alice G, *Beyond Sex Roles*, West Publishing Co. St Paul Minnesota, 1977.
6. Adapted from Stead, Bette Ann: *Women in Management*, Prentice Hall Inc, 1985.
7. Adapted from Back, K and K: *Assertiveness at Work*, McGraw Hill, 1982.
8. Bloom, LZ; Coburn, KP; Pearlman, J: *The New Assertive Woman*, Delacorte, 1975.
9. Berman Myrtle: *Freelance management and training consultant, 1986.*
10. *The Times*, 25 January 1988.
    'Increase in women employees fails to close earnings gap (1987 figures).'

Special courses for women

The New Assertive Woman Manager

British Institute of Management   0536 204222
Management House
Cottingham Road
CORBY
Northants
NN17 1TT

Strategies for the Successful Woman
For women who wish to make the
transition into the highest levels of
management.

Urwick Management Centre   0753 34111
Stoke Poges Lane
SLOUGH
SL1 3PF

Business Leadership for Women

Ashridge Management College   044284 3491
BERKHAMPSTEAD
Hertfordshire
HP4 1BR

For a variety of courses for women

Civil Service Courses   0990 23444
Sunningdale Park
ASCOT
Berks SL5 0QE

For in-company courses and individual
counselling

The author's company:

Denham-Nash   01–891 0033
Management Consultants   01–892 3339
22 Ailsa Road
TWICKENHAM
Middlesex
TW1 1QW

Lifestyle, stress and career counselling

Lifestyle Management Consultants   01–543 2086
13 Merton Hall Road
Wimbledon
LONDON
SW19 3PP

Stress counselling and healing

Brenda S Donald MPS   01–642 6046
41 Cadogan Court
Mulgrave Road
SUTTON
Surrey
SM2 6LN

Help with mid career stagnation and
difficulty

The Mid Career Development Centre   01–654 0808
77 Morland Road
CROYDON
Surrey
CR0 6EA

Financial planning consultants

Fiona Price and Partners   01–486 4822
Independent Financial Advisers
Suites 19 & 20
38 Wigmore Street
LONDON
W1H 9DF

Bower Banks & Company   01–790 4010
Wickham House
10 Cleveland Way
LONDON E1 4TR

Ante-natal and post-natal courses

Maternity Matters   01–673 1457
5 Culverden Road
Balham
LONDON
SW12 9LR

Assistance to small businesses

A Big Help to a Small Business   Dial 100 and ask for
A service by the Department of   Freephone Enterprise
Employment.

The Business Start Up Programme.
(A Home Study Course)

The Rapid Results College   01–947 7272
27/37 St Georges Road
LONDON
SW19 4DS

Colour analysis

House of Colour	01–581 3281
Your True Colours	04 482 2038
First Impressions	0223 462700
Colour Me Beautiful	01–627 5211
Academy of Colour and Style	0525 375041

Wardrobe advisory services

Harvey Nichols   01–235 5000
109–125 Knightsbridge
LONDON
SW1X 7RJ

Contact: Garbrielle De Nora
Personal Shopping Service available to all customers, provided by a team of 6 people with 2 'floaters'.

Selfridges   01–629 1234
400 Oxford Street
LONDON
W1 1AB

Contact: Mrs Scott Taylor, Press Office
Wardrobe Co-ordination Service

Wardrobe (Beautiful Clothes) Ltd   01–935 4086
17 Chiltern Street
LONDON W1M 1HE

3 Grosvenor Street   01–629 7044
LONDON W1X 9FA

Contact: Alex Poppleton
Wardrobe Consultancy Service. Initial 1hr–2hr consultation fee is deducted from the price of clothes bought.

Harrods   01–730 1234
Knightsbridge
LONDON
SW1X 7XL

Contact: Stella Burrows 01–581 4874
Executive Suite Service. A computerised comprehensive service.

Liberty   01–734 1234
210–220 Regent Street
LONDON
W1R 6AH

Contact: Liz Curd, extension 2341
Personal Charge Service. Not simply fashion, but tailored to
meet any requirements. This relatively new service is to be
computerised.

Dickins & Jones   01–734 7070
224 Regent Street
LONDON
W1A 1DB

Contact: Mary Cavanagh
Shopping Service that Mary Cavanagh has provided on a very
personal basis for 20 years!

Recommended reading

Back, K & K: *Assertiveness at Work*, McGraw Hill 1982.

Brownmiller, Susan: *Femininity*, Paladin Grafton Books 1986.

Bloom L Z; Coburn, K; Pearlman, J: *The New Assertive Woman*, Delacorte 1975.

Davidson, Marilyn: *Reach for the Top*, Piatkus 1985.

Dickson, Anne: *A Woman in Your Own Right*, Quartet 1982.

Dowling, Colette: *The Cinderella Complex*, Summit Books 1981; Fontana Paperbacks 1982.

Fezler, Wm. and Field, Eleanor: *The Good Girl Syndrome*, Thorsons 1988.

Friday, Nancy: *Jealousy*, Wm. Morrow 1985; Wm. Collins 1986; Fontana Paperbacks 1987.

Friday, Nancy: *My Mother Myself*, Fontana 1975.

Friedan, Betty: *The Feminine Mystique*, W. W. Norton 1963; Gollancz 1963; Penguin Books 1965.

Friedan, Betty: *The Second Stage*, Michael Joseph 1982; Sphere Books 1983.

Grice, Julia: *What Makes a Woman Sexy*, Piatkus 1988.

Harris, Amy & Thomas: *Staying OK*, Cape 1985; Pan Books 1986.

Josepowitz, N: *Paths to Power*, Columbus 1980.

Orbach, Susie: *Fat is a Feminist Issue*, Paddington Press 1978; Hamlyn Paperbacks 1984.

Orbach, Susie, and Eichenbaum, Luise: *Bittersweet*, Century Hutchinson 1987.

Stead, Bette Ann: *Women in Management*, Prentice-Hall Inc 1985.

Syrett, Michel, and Dunn, Chris: *Starting a Business on a Shoestring*, Penguin 1988.

Wallis, Margaret: *Getting There: Job Hunting for Women*, Kogan Page 1987.

Index